Pastoral Year
Notre Dame, Ind.

# St. Joseph and Daily Christian Living

## OTHER BOOKS BY FATHER FILAS

The Man Nearest to Christ
The Family for Families
Joseph and Jesus
His Heart in Our Work (ed.)
Joseph Most Just
The Parables of Jesus

# St. Joseph and Daily Christian Living

## Reflections on His Life and Devotion

Francis L. Filas, S.J.

New York
The Macmillan Company
1959

IMPRIMI POTEST: William J. Schmidt, S.J.
Provincial, Chicago Province,
Society of Jesus
January 6, 1959

NIHIL OBSTAT: Austin G. Schmidt, S.J.
Censor Librorum
January 13, 1959

IMPRIMATUR: ✠Albert G. Meyer
Archbishop of Chicago
January 15, 1959



First Printing

The Macmillan Company, New York
Brett-Macmillan Ltd., Galt, Ontario

Printed in the United States of America

Grateful acknowledgment is made to the following publishers for permission to quote from: *The Parish Priest* by Eugene Masure, Fides, Notre Dame, Ind.; *The Imitation of Christ,* J. S. Paluch Co., Chicago; *The Spiritual Life* by Adolphe Tanquerey, The Desclee Co., Inc., New York; *Marriage and the Family* by Alphonse H. Clemens, copyright 1957 by Prentice-Hall, Inc., New York; "The Accident of Birth," in *Fortune,* February, 1938.

New Testament quotations are generally taken from *The New Testament of Our Lord and Saviour Jesus Christ,* translated into English from the original Greek by the Very Rev. Francis Aloysius Spencer, O.P., edited by Charles J. Callan, O.P., and John A. McHugh, O.P. Copyright 1937 by The Macmillan Company and used by permission of The Macmillan Company.

Library of Congress catalog card number: 59–12339

# Contents

REFLECTIONS ABOUT ST. JOSEPH—WHY? vii

NOTE x

1. ST. JOSEPH'S VOCATION 1
The Lesson of Faith—God's Will—The Faith of Joseph and Mary

2. ST. JOSEPH'S FAMILY BACKGROUND 12
How Old Was St. Joseph?—Intelligent Piety Vs. Blind Devotion—Discouragement from Impossible Goals?—The Question of Perfection—"It Really Happened"

3. ST. JOSEPH'S MARRIAGE 33
The Love of Joseph and Mary—The Goodness of Marriage

4. ST. JOSEPH'S VIRGINITY 45
The Legends and Joseph's Virginity—The Goodness of Virginity

5. ST. JOSEPH'S DOUBT 57
Scrupulosity and Guilt—Discouragement Again—and Always?

6. ST. JOSEPH'S FATHERHOOD 75
Joseph's Fatherly Titles—Love That Rules Out Jealousy

7. ST. JOSEPH AND THE EXILE 88
The Star of the Magi—God's Providence—Joseph's Emotional Maturity

8. ST. JOSEPH'S TRUST 100
Conformity to God's Will—Confidence in God—The Joy of Joseph and Mary—Cheerfulness

9. THE HIDDEN LIFE 114
St. Joseph as Protector—Joseph's Trade—Zeal and the Hidden Life

10. ST. JOSEPH'S DEATH 124
Fears of Death—The Spirit of Gratitude

11. ST. JOSEPH AND THE POPES 135
*Quemadmodum Deus*—Pius IX 136
*Inclytum Patriarcham*—Pius IX 139
*Quamquam Pluries*—Leo XIII 141
*Neminem Fugit*—Leo XIII 150
*Bonum Sane*—Benedict XV 153
*Divini Redemptoris*—Pius XI 156
Two Tributes from Pius XI 157
Joseph the Worker—Pius XII 158
Prayer to Joseph the Worker—Pius XII 161
Radiocast to American Schoolchildren—Pius XII 162

12. ST. JOSEPH BEGINS TO COME INTO HIS OWN 165
Joseph's Dignity and Holiness—Joseph's Prerogatives—St. Joseph's Name in the Mass?

EPILOGUE: ST. JOSEPH AS I SEE HIM 175

TOPICAL INDEX 181

# Reflections About St. Joseph—Why?

This book presents two types of material: facts about the life and devotion to St. Joseph, and reflections that grow out of them. These reflections are intended to be as universal as possible in their application. They are based on history and dogma and ascetical theology, not on legends, private revelations, or pious fancy. Often enough, as we begin with an episode in the life of St. Joseph, our thoughts will develop into considerations far removed from the original topic. None the less, there will always be the logical growth of an idea linked to some event or characteristic in the unusual career of a most unusual saint.

For many people the idea of reflections on the life of a saint is already set by experience. It brings to mind pious essays in which an author presents pet opinions of his own and uses the life of the saint as the occasion for doing so. This is the type of "reflection" which loves to indulge in the "he must have often . . ." sentence. Such reconstructions are not completely out of place. When we know the general customs of a past era, we are certainly correct in supposing that a citizen of that time would act in such a way. But beyond this, we cannot justify claims that involve details which are farfetched and impossible to verify.

Generally speaking, the more material that exists concerning the life of a saint, so much the less leeway exists for purely subjective opinions. On the other hand, the less historical material the author has, so much the more latitude for his imagination to run wild. In the case of some of the older "lives" of St. Joseph, it was easy for them to fall into the habit of building up reflections that had little foundation in reality. Their excuse was that they were filling in the gaps of scanty historical data. The story is told (probably it is apocryphal) about the St. Joseph book that was supposedly developed from one sentence in the gospel of Matthew, "He was a just man." The rest of the book, so the story goes, devoted itself to a study of what the typical just man must be, and then claimed that everything the typical just man would do in any given circumstance was actually done by St. Joseph.

A tale of this sort tends to discredit devotion to St. Joseph, as if the devotion had to be unreliable because we know relatively so little about the Saint. It does point up the need for placing the devotion on as solid and scholarly a basis as possible. Knowledge can lead to love, and love always asks for more knowledge. Our devotion normally increases in proportion to our knowledge, and the more devotion we have toward St. Joseph, so much the more do we desire to know more about him. Once we know more about him, we can discern ever more clearly how we can imitate his example in our lives. The best sign of our love is the imitation of his love for Jesus and for Mary.

The reflections that follow are written for men and women in any walk of life. They are particularly intended to have special value for people who are worried and who need positive encouragement. Such individuals are often uneasy because they realize how far their life seems to fall short of what it should be in God's sight. They feel their spiritual "failure" too keenly. Their discouragement bogs down much of their effort toward the essentials of spiritual success.

For all its good will their attitude is not the ideal nor is it necessarily correct. Thousands of such persons wanting to serve God lose the benefit of knowing the good they are doing and the good they can do, because of misplaced emphasis on their failings, whether real or imagined. They are worriers throughout. Feelings of doubt and insecurity in various forms pervade their outlook.

If you are one of these, this book does not intend to make you apathetic or complacent with your actual shortcomings. That would be unfair to you, for it would not be seeking your best interest. Far from wanting to hinder the desire to do good, it is dedicated to increase in you your love of God, but to do it peaceably. The one thing it wishes to remove is an obstacle—not necessarily the obstacle of openly recognized selfishness, but the hidden obstacles of misunderstanding some of the *positive* aspects of the spiritual life. It is written to help you see the goodness of God in yourself and in your life, to encourage you, under the leadership and intercession of St. Joseph to be more perfect, with ever greater peace of God in your heart.

Precisely here comes the value of the material concerning St. Joseph's life and items of interest in devotion to him. We are not looking at an abstract plan of living, but have an attractive personal model before our eyes. Moreover, the constant shifting of the emphasis in the following pages from St. Joseph to ourselves and back to St. Joseph serves as something of an antidote to an overweening sense of importance whereby our spiritual life and its interests would become some sort of pet hobby, instead of a whole-souled dedication to *God* and *His* interests. That is one of the reasons why St. Joseph holds the center of the stage in what follows here.

This book is Joseph's, in deepest gratitude; and through him is humbly given to Mary and to Jesus.

FRANCIS L. FILAS, S. J., S.T.D.

Loyola University
Chicago, Illinois
Feast of the Holy Name of Jesus
1959

# Note

New Testament quotations are in general from the Spencer translation. Translations of the papal documents are from the following sources:

*Quemadmodum Deus.* Except for editorial emendations, from the *Dublin Review,* 16 (1871), January.

*Inclytum Patriarcham.* Author's translation of Decree No. 3252 of the Congregation of Sacred Rites.

*Quamquam Pluries.* Author's translation from *Acta Sanctae Sedis,* 22, 65.

*Neminem Fugit.* Author's translation of sections of Decree No. 3777 of the Congregation of Sacred Rites.

*Bonum Sane.* Except for editorial emendations, from the *Catholic Mind,* September 22, 1920.

*Divini Redemptoris.* Extract from official English text issued by the Vatican Polyglot press and printed in the *Catholic Mind,* April 22, 1937.

Discourse of Pius XI, March 19, 1928. Author's translation from *Vie Spirituelle,* 19 (1928–1929), 677–678.

Discourse of Pius XI, March 19, 1935. Author's translation from *Bollettino del clero romano,* 16 (1935), 57.

Institution of feast of Joseph the Worker. Except for editorial emendations, from *Catholic Documents* (London: Salesian Press), No. 18, July, 1955. *Acta Apostolicae Sedis* 47 (1955), 402.

Prayer of Pius XII in honor of Joseph the Worker. Author's translation from French text in *Cahiers de Josephologie,* 6 (1958), 118, reproducing French edition of *Osservatore Romano,* March 28, 1958. *Acta Apostolicae Sedis* 50 (1958), 174.

Pius XII, radiocast to American schoolchildren. English text printed in *Cahiers de Josephologie,* 6 (1958), 117–118, reproducing *Osservatore Romano,* February 20, 1958. *Acta Apostolicae Sedis* 50 (1958), 335.

# 1.
# St. Joseph's Vocation

Words usually lose their full impact when they are repeated over and over, as everyday experience proves. Something of this process has occurred in the case of the word "vocation." We have used it so much in so many different senses that we lose the force of its first meaning. We speak of vocational guidance, of one's vocation in life, and of a "vocation" in the special sense of a life dedicated to God. But these are all derivations of the root meaning of the word. A vocation is not primarily one's life or career. First and foremost, it is one's *calling* from God our Creator, who in His providence offers to each of us certain circumstances amid which we are to work out our welfare.

St. Joseph's vocation, then, was God's call according to God's plan. The fascinating thing about it all is that Joseph himself was unaware for long years of what God had in store for him. From our perspective of almost twenty centuries we are able to discern how Joseph was to fit within the plan.

The human race was to be redeemed, and this was to be done by a Savior not merely human but divine as well. Still more, this was not to be brought about in a spectacular manner to the accompaniment of constant miracles and angelic trumpets from heaven. Instead, it was to be accomplished in great measure according to the ordinary laws of everyday life. The Savior was to be born into the world like any other child and live a life of obscurity until the time divinely predetermined, when He was to preach the fact of His divine origin and the contents of His divine message. Then and only then, after His teaching and preaching message was finished, would God providentially allow the forces of evil to wipe out, apparently forever, all the success and hope of the God-man's work by means of what seemed to be a most crushing defeat. The apparent defeat, of course, was to be turned into an even greater and more glorious victory by means of the Resurrection, but this was to come only after the obscurity, humiliation, pain, and poverty of His life on earth.

Where did Joseph fit into this picture? God had planned that the Second Person of the Blessed Trinity should take on Himself human nature. As a particular sign and proof of the fact that Jesus was divine, He would accomplish this by the miracle of beginning His human life in the womb of a virgin mother, "and the virgin's name was Mary." Something more was involved. God had also decreed that, as far as possible, the birth and rearing of the Child Jesus were to follow the laws of human life as He had already established them in the world. In other words Jesus was to come into the world in the midst of a human family.

For this part of the plan the cooperation of St. Joseph was necessary. Only a man of superlative virtue would have been worthy enough to become the husband of the Virgin Mary and to act as the father of the Child Jesus on this earth. God followed His own law of marriage by willing that the Child should come into the world within the bonds of marriage, even though this entrance was miraculous. Moreover, the Child was to be like every other child in craving the security and the love of a father and mother, "One tried in all things like ourselves," Paul can insistently remind us, "yet sinless" (Heb. 4:15). As far as we can pierce the depths of the divine counsel, the reason for the virginity of Mary's motherhood ultimately lay in the fact that it was the miraculous proof of the divine origin of Jesus. The virginal motherhood simultaneous with conception within marriage could only mean the existence of a virginal marriage.

This called, therefore, for a husband willing to love his wife with a wholly self-sacrificing love that would never ask for the fulfillment of the marriage privilege, a man who would protect his wife Mary's virginity. It called, too, for the husband to have a holiness commensurate with the dignity of the position he held. He would be in the closest contact with the holiest of all God's creatures, Mary. Later, after the first Christmas he would be living under the same roof as God in human flesh. He would be chosen by God to give the God-child the name that was above all other names. He would be chosen to command God as his son on earth. He was to love Mary as his wife and to love Jesus as his son, with spiritual ties closer than existed in any other marriage on this earth.

That was the life to which God called St. Joseph. From it stemmed the requirements of St. Joseph's vocation. All the evidence indicates that Joseph knew nothing of what God had in store for him. Here we begin to see how the plans of God work when He asks for the cooperation of His creatures.

In the case of St. Joseph as in the case of our Lady, God did not let them know from the beginning of their conscious lives that they were to be the ones most intimately connected with the Incarnation, and therefore with the Redemption. The evidence is clearly contained in the gospel accounts. Before the Annunciation, Mary certainly had no inkling that she was to be the mother of the Messiah and the Mother of God. Otherwise, she would not have been so surprised at the angelic visitation. The angel's message would have been practically unnecessary.

So, too, in the case of St. Joseph. A message of an angel was necessary to let him know that Mary his wife had miraculously conceived. Only from that message could he learn his part in his calling as head of the Holy Family.

## The Lesson of Faith

The lesson for us is that God does not call us by angelic silver trumpets or flashing visions of spiritual insight, although in certain rare cases (as He eventually did for Joseph and Mary) He may make use of some sort of extraordinary intimation of His will. We can never forget that even in the case of these two chosen souls who had the most sublime vocations ever given human beings, God did not let them know from the beginning what they were to be.

We can discern a sort of economy in the divine message. They are told as much as they have to know—that is sufficient, as God determines it. The rest is to be learned by means of the ordinary channels of finding God's will: the duties of one's state of life, and the changing events as God permits them to happen to us and thus to shape the course of our future.

With us it seems to be a not uncommon reaction to feel somewhat resentful against God for putting such a plan into the world. We feel that if we had been the Creator, things would have been arranged differently and (implicitly we add) much better, too. In our human plan for a reorganized universe the grace of God would not be dispensed in what seems so scanty a measure. People would not be told only as much as they have to know; they would be told more. They would not have to undergo the trial of finding God's will by the ordinary channels: the duties of their state of life or the changing events that befall them, together with all the doubts that assail them in the process. They would be given clear, definite signals, with no obscurity involved in learning God's will.

Our plan for this brave new world continues. There would be no instances of souls who are apparently not much in God's favor, to judge by the dearth of gifts in their lives. There would also be more awareness of God by means of more direct contact with the Creator, known and experienced as such. We would be freed from the necessities of making blind acts of faith, especially concerning the apparent evidence that God dispenses His gifts with special favor for some and disdain for others. This is always a difficulty for us, whether we look at the inequality of the temporal gifts of health and talents, or the spiritual gifts of virtue that come so easily for some, yet so hard for others. The worst difficulty concerns the moral and religious exile of the benighted millions who never had the chance to be taught God's word.

Such seems to be a rather fair presentation of our problems with the divine plan of the universe, together with our human idea on reworking it. But now let us compare it to the present system, correctly understood. Would any change actually be toward an improvement, or would any such change make us happier?

When we analyze the difficulty carefully, at the root it is simply a lack of faith in God's providence and wisdom and goodness. When you and I have wonderings in this way, we are doing nothing else but wondering why God has decided to lead us by blind faith, or we are even complaining because He has decided to do so. To live by faith takes exertion and means sacrifice. Perhaps that is why we do not like it.

If we examine each of the difficulties that occur to us in this regard, we will find that an answer from faith will solve them all. I do not say that we will know what the full and explicit answer will ultimately be; but I do say we will know that such an answer exists.

For example, *is* the grace of God actually dispensed in so scanty a measure? We have no right to say this because we have no experience of realities of the supernatural order, in the sense that we must believe that they exist but with our natural faculties we do not recognize them in our lives. Moreover, we have no knowledge of precisely how God will judge His creatures, but we do know that His justice and mercy will far exceed any norm of justice and mercy we could ourselves set down. That can only mean that the final answer, whenever we arrive at it, will be completely satisfactory.

As to the claim that people should have a clearer idea of what is coming, again the difficulty is ultimately one of faith; there can be no camouflage of what is lacking here. Eventually we will discover the facts: It has been for our best welfare that we were kept in the darkness of faith.

The comparison has often been used that when we live by faith in God, we are blindfolded children being led along mountain paths. Blindfolded children in such a case would not know where they are, but they would be equally ignorant of the yawning abysses they avoided. The one certain fact remains that they would be safe, for God is their guide. Thus again, every time objections rise in our hearts against the necessity of faith, their force disappears under closer scrutiny. At some time in the future we will discover why God has willed to use the plans He has chosen. For the present we must simply be obedient and accept in silence what the Creator has determined for our own good. If God was good enough and strong and wise enough to make us, does He not have sufficient goodness and strength and wisdom to keep us in existence?

This need of faith in God is all so logical because faith is the foundation of all our other virtues. If we do not believe in what God has promised us, we can have no hope or love. Without faith, too, we lack the spark of a principle to lead us to action. Faith, whether in God or in man, always means that we take the word of someone else. We go forward according to information we have learned not by our own experience but because someone told us it was so.

Even though the braggart atheist can boast of his independence of faith, he is actually contradicting himself. Such a man can deliberately put faith in God out of his life, but he cannot stop accepting the word of his fellow men. He continues to live on faith in man at the same time he is boasting of his freedom from faith in God. No one can live one day without taking the word of another.

The news brought to our doorstep by modern agencies of communication is accepted on faith. We take the word of the witness, the reporter, the editor, the newspaper that it is so. We accept the claim of the store clerk that food for our life is what it is claimed to be and not poison instead. For that matter, every label on a commercial product affords us an occasion to exercise faith. We accept the statement of the manufacturer as to the nature and quality of his product, as well as the diagnosis of the physician as to whether we need drastic surgery. In all such cases these are statements which practically none of us can verify from our own experience, or which only a few could verify after long and expensive study.

A logical parallel exists between this natural faith in human beings and what should be our supernatural faith in God. On the one hand we accept the testimony of man, who can be deceived and who can deceive us. We trust our health, our fortunes, our families, our very lives to human authority. Should we not trust the testimony of God at least to an equal degree, since God cannot deceive or be deceived?

In theory the logic is irrefutable. God's word should be accepted if for no other reason than the fact that we are willing to accept the word of man. In practice, however, we feel much differently about it. The reason is that now we are dealing with truths of a supernatural and immaterial order. In that milieu we feel reluctant to humble ourselves before the word of God.

The solution? There is only one adequate answer: "Lord, I believe. Help my unbelief!" It is a question here of submission of our intellect to the word of God. We must humble human knowledge before the knowledge of the Creator, who knows better than we do what is good for us. We cannot justifiably allege the excuse that it is sometimes hard to find what God wishes us to believe. Such situations do occur where the facts are difficult to ascertain or when the application of the moral law is not immediately clear. But in these cases, if and when they happen, we are free to withold belief until such time as the evidence of God's will again becomes clear. In most instances of human life, we have every reason to be certain of what God wishes in our regard. Of this we should be fully aware. How can we get such certainty?

## God's Will

There is a twofold answer to this question, according to the distinction that is made to help us understand the two types of God's will for us—or perhaps we should call these the two different channels whereby we learn God's will.

The first is what is called God's signified will. This consists of the duties of our state of life as we learn them from the Ten Commandments, the laws of the Church, and the ordinances of legitimate authority. In these instances we can have little doubt about the moral principles involved, little or no excuse on our part to claim that we ordinarily do not know what God wishes us to do. Even when commands come from legitimate human authority, these call for our obedience to such a superior unless the commands are manifestly sinful. We do not mean in these instances of obedience to humans that God would give precisely the same commands if He were in the place of humans, but we do mean that God wishes us to obey lawful authority, and this the more seriously as the commands are more serious and the matter is more grave.

The second method of knowing God's will is called God's will of good pleasure. This refers to events that happen to us. By the very fact that they have occurred, we are certain that in some sense or other they have been willed by God. We can be as sure of this fact as we are sure that God is the Creator. If anything occurred outside His permission, He would cease being ruler of the world, and that is an impossibility. Even the most distressing pain, failure, and suffering—for that matter, even the worst sin on our part or on the part of others—all this can happen only with God's permission. This is a true sense of God's will. We are perfectly logical in developing internal obedience to it as a means of becoming more closely conformed to God's will. Always we know that if He permitted it, He had some reason. God and God alone will be able to draw good even out of evil.

These two forms of God's will (in our way of thinking) possess differing characteristics. God's signified will is known ahead of time, because we know the right and wrong of the moral law long before the event occurs in which we are to apply the law. On the other hand, God's will of good pleasure can be known only by the fact that the event has occurred.

In the case of God's signified will we have the option of granting or withholding our external obedience. In the case of God's will of good pleasure, no such option exists. One cannot avoid accepting exteriorly what has actually happened. We can control only our inward submission.

Again, we can grow spiritually proud of our conformity to God's signified will, preening ourselves on our spiritual virtues and on our fidelity to God's law as we plan to follow it. But in the case of God's will of good pleasure such spiritual conceit is difficult. One can hardly become arrogant over the fact that an event was accepted because it happened. Nevertheless, the certainty is ever there: "What has happened to me, has happened because God willed it."

Still another difference between God's signified will and God's will of good pleasure is the fact that imprudent excesses can easily occur in the case of the one but hardly in the case of the other. By misunderstanding, ignorance, rashness, or spiritual pride one might fancy this or that exaggeration would be actually the correct path to follow. In this way health and sanity could suffer grave injury from injudicious fastings or penances, or from resolutions that far exceed normal powers of human endurance. Such dangers cannot take place in the case of God's will of good pleasure. The reason again is the same. Conformity here means the acceptance of what has already happened.

There is, of course, the condition laid down by prudence: *Provided we have done what we ought, in accordance with God's signified will,* we should rest content and accept the outcome as God's will of good pleasure. This prudence in conformity to God's will extends even further. We would not be justified in adopting a policy of slothful apathy, refusing to plan or labor for any course of action for the future because after all, God will decide what will happen, no matter what we do. Planning for the future and working according to our capacity is expected of us according to right reason, biblical doctrine, and legitimate teachers in the Church.

"Man proposes, God disposes." In this respect the time-honored proverb has a very correct application. According to God's signified will man "proposes," following the lights of his own conscience formed by the moral law; but God "disposes" according to His will of good pleasure following His all-wise providence governing every detail of our lives.

One caution should be mentioned in connection with conformity to God's will of good pleasure. We should not minutely inspect each detail in our lives, trying to see where and how the pattern of providence will show itself. The reason is that in no case can we embrace the entire plan and the entire picture. It is too vast for us to grasp.

## The Faith of Joseph and Mary

Both Joseph and Mary were kept ignorant of this pattern of providence until the time when God gradually began to reveal it to them. Yet they were prepared for it when it came, even though they had not explicitly known what it might be.

In secular careers preparation for future work implies and requires a full knowledge of the work concerned. In fact, the more detailed a study one can make, so much the more will one know what will be expected. In the case of conformity to God's will, however, this knowledge of the future is neither required nor is it usually given by God. Instead, the preparation develops not by knowledge of what will be asked of us but by a sincere desire to please God in each action of the moment. Only thus can we make ourselves less unworthy instruments to do what God wishes in our state of life, no matter how humble and unassuming our task may seem to be.

We mentioned earlier that until Mary and Joseph received their individual messages from the angel, God kept them ignorant of the nature of their calling. It is imperative to add that after each of them had been thus initiated into the mystery of the Incarnation, even then they did not know fully what was expected of them.

Several events of the gospel story make this clear. When the Magi came to Bethlehem, an angel told Joseph to take the Child and His mother to Egypt—but for how long, Joseph was not told. On the return, the information again merely concerned the return to Palestine—but precisely where and for how long, again Joseph was not told.

When the parents of Jesus lost the Child in the temple some years later through no fault of their own, they were given no divine intimation beforehand that this was to happen. They knew the Old Testament prophecies that the Messiah was to be a man of sorrows, but they did not know how these were to be accomplished. For all that Joseph and Mary could guess, the loss of the twelve-year-old Jesus was the beginning of whatever sorrows God had destined for His redemptive career.

This pattern of faith, with the gradual unfolding of God's plan only as events transpired, continued throughout the Hidden and Public Life as well. Jesus lived quietly at Nazareth for practically thirty years. Until His Father's will would call Him to public preaching, the consummation of His sufferings would wait, but we have no indication that either Mary or Joseph knew when that hour would come.

It is most consoling to us ordinary and sinful humans to see how God follows out this plan of blind faith with even His nearest and dearest saints—Mary and Joseph, the two holiest of all. They could practice conformity to the divine will only in blind faith, just as we are to do. They knew from their consciences and from scripture the divine signified will of how they were to live. As each day brought its light or its darkness into their lives, they saw the loving hand of the Eternal Father behind everything that transpired. The example is before our eyes to be copied.

# 2.
# St. Joseph's Family Background

The story of anyone's life reminds us that others are made of the same flesh and blood as we are, with its weaknesses and its strengths. Personal details interest us even more when they concern someone we love. In the case of St. Joseph the personal details serve their purpose of emphasizing his humanness.

Very little evidence exists concerning St. Joseph's early life. His ancestry was of the house of David, as Matthew and Luke tell us; his birthplace was probably Bethlehem. The reason for such a supposition is that he took Mary to Bethlehem for the census on the occasion of the first Christmas. Several years later, his first thought on leaving the exile in Egypt was again to return to Bethlehem. From this it is logical to conclude that he or his family owned property there; it is equally logical to believe that there he had been born.

Joseph is mentioned in the genealogy of our Lord because through Joseph, Jesus received His legal ancestry. Matthew says that Joseph is the son of Jacob (1:16); Luke says he is the son of Heli (3:23). This brings up the celebrated difficulty of how Joseph could have had two fathers, Jacob and Heli. Certainly, neither of the evangelists is in error. Even apart from the fact that the divinely inspired gospel text cannot present an erroneous judgment as its own, continued research corroborates again and again the data of the gospels. Hence, there must be some other answer to the problem.

Various solutions have been suggested. The most likely one is based on the Jewish custom of the levirate marriage (Deut. 25:5). This law had been put into effect so that a man's name would not die out from the genealogy of his people. When a husband died childless, so the law stated, the brother of the dead husband was to marry his widow. The first child of the new union was to be *legally* the son of the first husband, even though he was the *natural* son of the second marriage.

According to the application of this law in the case of St. Joseph, Jacob was the natural father of Joseph, and Heli the legal father. In the supposition Heli had married Joseph's mother and then died without issue. Jacob, Heli's half-brother, then took Heli's widow as his wife, and their first child was St. Joseph. But since the ancestors of Jacob are listed differently in Matthew's gospel than the ancestors of Heli as listed in Luke, a further suggestion has been made to overcome this further difficulty. Jacob and Heli had a common mother, who bore Heli in her first marriage. After becoming a widow, she remarried and bore Jacob to her second husband, who was, however, no relation to the first. Schematically,

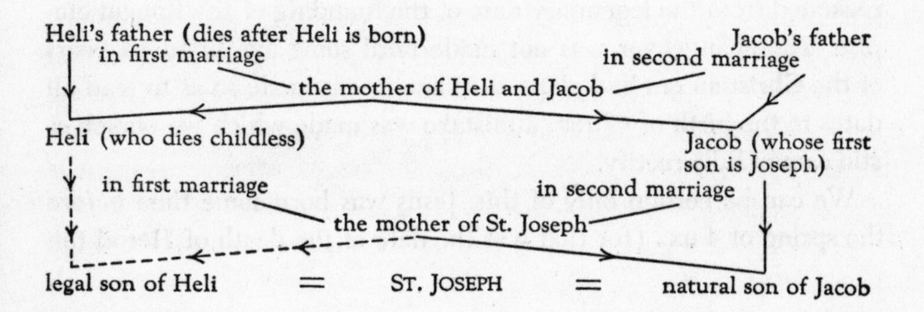

This solution of the double genealogy of St. Joseph cannot be considered absolutely certain. None the less, it seems to be the most probable among the various answers proposed by commentators on the gospel, and much more so than the claim that the genealogies are merely literary forms, devoid of historical basis.

A few other statements are found in Christian history that supposedly give us the names of relatives of St. Joseph. Probably the only reliable testimony is the early comment (quoted from Hegesippus by the Church historian Eusebius of Caesarea) that "Clopas" was the brother of our St. Joseph. This Clopas is mentioned as the husband (or the father?) of a Mary who stood with our Lady at the foot of the cross on Calvary (Jn. 19:25).

## How Old Was St. Joseph?

The date of St. Joseph's birth cannot be learned directly since no trace of any such record exists. Instead, we argue from the probable age of St. Joseph at the time he was espoused to our Lady. Since this in turn is connected with the date of the first Christmas, we suggest that St. Joseph was born about 25 B.C. The links in this series of deductions make up a long chain, but even though they can give us only probable evidence, their results are far better than the other alternative of silence.

To begin with, our modern calendar is in error. When we call the years of our era by the title *Anno Domini*, A.D., "the year of our Lord," we are not historically accurate. Early Christians calculated their years according to the "A.U.C." system (*ab urbe condita*), which reckoned from the legendary date of the founding of the Roman empire. The changeover was not made until some five hundred years of the Christian era had elapsed. When it was made so as to lead all dates to the birth of Christ, a mistake was made which we ourselves still cannot fully rectify.

We can be certain only of this. Jesus was born some time *before* the spring of 4 B.C. (for that was the date of the death of Herod the

Great, who was living when the first Christmas occurred); and some time *after* 8 B.C. (for that was the approximate date when the Roman census was first proclaimed, as mentioned by Luke in his Christmas story). Further considerations of the time of the visit of the Magi, the age of Jesus when He began His Public Life, and the shepherds' all-night vigil on Christmas night suggest the lambing season, spring, in 6 B.C. as the most probable date of our Lord's birth.

This would place the Annunciation of our Lady nine months earlier, in about June of 7 B.C. Since the Annunciation occurred probably in the eighth month of Mary's espousal to St. Joseph (as we shall explain in a later chapter), we deduce that the espousal might have taken place about November of 8 B.C.

The discovery of the Dead Sea scrolls has unfolded the knowledge of many old Jewish customs concerning which we were hitherto ignorant. From them we learn that the conservative sect of the Essenes taught that a man should postpone his marriage till he is at least twenty years old. In other words the age of twenty was later than usual. This confirms rabbinical data suggesting that a man should be espoused before his eighteenth or nineteenth year. If we apply these findings to St. Joseph, his espousal in 8 B.C. would indicate that he had been born about 25 B.C.

However, this conclusion that Joseph was no more than eighteen when he married our Lady clashes violently with the centuries-old "popular tradition" that the Saint was advanced in years at the time of the espousal. So many interesting and important factors concerning St. Joseph and the devotion to him are connected with this question of his age that it is worth our while to study the facts at some length.

The gospel witness does not give explicit support to the thesis of Joseph's many years. However, because of its silence on the subject, it could be interpreted as permitting the impression that the "old" St. Joseph was in accord with the rest of the narrative.

The first sources for the idea of Joseph's age are three or four apocryphal legends concerning the childhood of Jesus. These legends, we must note, are pious tales which expanded on the gospel story. It is theoretically possible that originally they included some traces of correct tradition not contained in the gospels; but as time went on, they were worked over and enlarged to such an extent that no competent scholar would claim them now as reliable direct evidence. Indirectly, of course, they are valuable because they mirror the beliefs of their times. The legends were created to fill a need, namely, to satisfy pious curiosity concerning the gaps in the gospel narrative. Some of the apocrypha of this type had heretical leanings and were composed to further the cause of heterodoxy by posing as "fifth gospels." The ones with which we are concerned here are for the most part orthodox.

The first reference to St. Joseph's extreme age is found in the so-called *Protoevangel of James,* which was in circulation by A.D. 150. It is almost six thousand words long in English translation (equivalently twenty double-spaced typewritten pages), and covers the period from the prayer of Mary's parents, begging God to give them children, up to the murder of the Holy Innocents. As its name indicates, its author is claimed to be the apostle St. James the Less. It ascribes these words to Joseph:

"I have children and I am an old man, and she is a young girl. I am afraid lest I become a laughing-stock to the sons of Israel."

This idea was developed in another legend some three centuries later, which modern scholars call the *Gospel of Pseudo-Matthew* (incidentally more than twice as long as its prototype):

"Whence it happened that Joseph brought his rod together with the young men . . . but because he was an old man, he had been cast off."

And again: "[Joseph said] 'I am an old man and have children; why do you hand me over to this infant, who is younger than my grandsons?' "

And finally: "Then all the people congratulated the old man, saying, 'Thou hast been made blessed in thy old age, O father Joseph.' "

The theme for the legends was now well formed. We are not

surprised to find the fantastic figures in the Coptic *History of Joseph the Carpenter* that Joseph married at forty, became a widower at eighty-nine, received Mary as his ward at ninety-one, and died at the ripe old age of one hundred and eleven!

The Middle Ages witnessed a tremendous upsurge of piety concerning the person of Christ. That brought with it equal interest in Mary, and so it was that Joseph could hardly be kept out of the picture. The medievals, of course, did not find all the details they wished to have from the gospel narrative. Their long poetic lives of Jesus accordingly fell back on the apocryphal legends for material. Thus the aged St. Joseph was woven into the popular devotional picture of the Holy Family. These medieval lives, incidentally, rejected almost all of the bizarre and coarse elements of the legends but heightened the romantic beauty of what they kept. So it was that much material was retained which was charming and warm and pleasing to the devout hearts of its time. Unfortunately, this was an uncritical acceptance whose effects we still sense in our devotional literature today.

We must recall, too, that up to the Middle Ages no such thing as formal devotion to St. Joseph existed in the Church. (By "devotion" is meant here a special emphasis on the Saint as an important cooperator in the Incarnation of our Lord and therefore in the Redemption.) The obscurity of Joseph helped to perpetuate the "old" St. Joseph. The very fact that he had been given so little notice meant that people did not understand the sublime heights of his vocation, surpassed by none except that of our Lady.

Because they did not know his vocation, they could hardly evaluate him properly and thus had no hesitation in consigning him to the very minimum position possible that could still be reconciled with the requirements of the gospel narrative: a character incidental to the story of the Incarnation. They were not conditioned to reason that a picture of the old St. Joseph contradicted the vocation of the true St. Joseph. The same hesitancy that had kept the Saint completely in the background for so many centuries still operated to keep him partially in the background as a senile "extra" on the stage. True, the portrayal of the stereotyped ancient was an improvement, but by no means did this remove the earlier neglect.

The reasons for these long centuries of Joseph's obscurity help us appreciate all the more the open freedom of the Saint's devotion today. In the infant Church most of the emphasis in honoring the saints was directed to martyrs, in view of the atmosphere of persecutions then so prevalent. Joseph was not recorded as a martyr, and he seemed to belong to the Old Testament of preparation, not the New Testament of fulfillment.

Then, too, the rash of heresies against the Blessed Trinity and the Incarnation engaged all the forces of churchmen. They had to fight to safeguard the essentials of the Faith. We can reasonably understand that they would have little time or energy to devote to a saint whose position could so easily be misunderstood.

Here lies the main reason for the delay in appreciating St. Joseph's true dignity. In the case of our Lady, Mary's cultus was manifestly linked with the honor of Jesus. In the present order of God's providence Mary's virginal motherhood helped as a proof of Christ's divinity and could hardly be looked upon as anything else. In the case of St. Joseph, however, his position regarding Mary and Jesus was liable to be regarded as ambiguous. When heretics clamored that Jesus was not divine, that He was a natural son of a wife who used her marriage rights with her husband, the Fathers of the Church understandably kept Joseph in the background. Joseph's position as the virginal husband of Mary (and therefore as father of Jesus in the spiritual and not the physical order) was too vulnerable, too easy to misrepresent.

Fortunately, our own age has seen the free proclamation of St. Joseph's unique fatherhood. The precautionary silence of early centuries has long since outlived its usefulness—if indeed it had any. We can reject the obscurity of St. Joseph with the same force as we deny forthright his advanced age at the time he married our Lady. The evidence is strong.

As for his supposed age, we already mentioned that the gospels do not give the slightest hint that Joseph was advanced in years. We mentioned, too, that the apocryphal legends loved to portray details as historical in order to attain a religious goal. Their aim was ultimately polemic and not historical. They wished to appear as edifying literature, as is evident from even a surface reading of their contents. Their constant emphasis on the virginity of Mary shows how strongly the Christians of their era believed in the virginity of our Lady.

The legends wanted to protect at all costs the dogma of Mary's virginity and therefore of Christ's godhead. They went so far as to deny the existence of a genuine marriage between Mary and Joseph, depicting our Lady merely as Joseph's ward contrary to the gospel evidence. They were so eager to show forth Jesus as the omnipotent wonder worker that they abounded in tales of supposed miracles that strain the limits of delicacy and good taste no less than credulity.

For the legends, Joseph became a character who was expendable. He was to be described in such a way as to permit no doubt of the fact that he did not generate Jesus from Mary, and that he did not make use of his marriage rights with our Lady. What better description could be given to prove this than to give him the advanced years that would mean declining vigor and dead physical passion? Thus, the legends reasoned, no one could imagine that so decrepit a man could have been the natural father of Jesus. They forgot to take into account the fact that God's grace was a help in preserving Joseph's virginity far greater than any natural limitations of an aging body.

The main trouble with this characterization was that it destroyed the very truths it had been invented to save. If Joseph had been so old that he was physically incapable of generating Jesus, then Mary would have appeared as an adulteress in the public eye, and Jesus would have been suspected as an illegitimate son! We know from the gospel accounts that the Pharisees bitterly hated Jesus and sought every means of reviling His reputation. They criticized the lowliness of His origin but never once hinted at any impropriety. If anything, they took it for granted that he was the natural son of the family of

Joseph the carpenter, and therefore they assumed He could not be the divine ambassador He claimed to be. "The Jews therefore murmured about Him . . . And they kept saying, 'Is not this Jesus, the son of Joseph, whose father and mother we know?'" (Jn. 6:41–42).

Joseph, moreover, had to be vigorous enough to make the wearying trip into Egyptian exile with Mary and Jesus, and strong enough to support them for most of the thirty years of the Hidden Life. On all these scores we can only conclude that if Joseph had been so old a husband of Mary, his presence would have made the Holy Family most conspicuous instead of giving the secret of the Incarnation the protection and concealment God wished it to have.

This conclusion means that according to the requirements of St. Joseph's vocation as described in the gospels, the Saint was at the normal age for marrying our Lady. The Holy Family was taken for granted according to the customs of the time. The customs of the time were that Joseph should have been in his middle teens when he was espoused to our Lady. Mary in her turn would be two to three years younger than her virginal husband.

All this logic is given sound confirmation by the context of Luke's gospel. Luke mentions six persons in his narrative relating to the birth of Christ: Zachary, Elizabeth, Anna, Simeon, Mary, and Joseph. He explicitly depicts Zachary, Elizabeth, and Anna as advanced in years. By quoting Simeon's expectation of death after years of waiting to see the Messiah, Luke implies that Simeon, too, was aged. For Mary and Joseph, no such explicit or implicit reference to advanced age appears. Instead, the two are taken for granted as a typical husband and typical wife, beginning their lives together evidently at the marriageable age of young people which was usual in their country and century.

The modern acceptance of St. Joseph as a young man of normal marriageable age might well be styled a triumph of enlightened, intelligent piety over blind devotion. The story of the senile Joseph had been invented by the early legends with little or no regard how this could be squared with the full tenor of the gospel narrative. As the centuries progressed, the force of intellectual argument slowly drove back the old tradition. So rarely do we see an "old" Joseph in modern art that we can say the victory is complete today. Even in the statues and portraits which seem to make him overly mature, such an impression is gained more because of the beard he is wearing than any effort on the part of the artist or sculptor to depict advanced age. On this point religious logic has won out over illogical religious emotion.

## Intelligent Piety Vs. Blind Devotion

This conflict between the two impressions of St. Joseph's age can be used to exemplify the conflict between too much will—unmitigated voluntarism, and too much mind—radical intellectualism—in religious attitudes. Both approaches ought to go hand in hand, balancing each other without trespass. Both are essential for properly developed faith. If faith becomes too intellectual, it is cold, sterile, haughty. It can easily become hypocritical, too, mouthing principles which are never put into action because the will is not being used for good.

This hyperintellectualism is what the author of the *Imitation of Christ* criticized when he wrote, "What good is it to be able to explain the doctrine of the Blessed Trinity if you displease the Blessed Trinity by your lack of humility? It is a good life that makes you pleasing to God, not high-sounding words and clever expressions. It is better to feel contrition for your sins than to know how to define it. What good is it to know the entire bible by heart and to learn the sayings of all the philosophers if you live without grace and the love of God?" (1,1).

"Do not be overly anxious to learn too much, for great distraction and delusion are found in that. Intellectuals like to appear wise, but there are many things they study which do not benefit their souls in the least" (1,2). "Why trouble yourself about the fine points of philosophy, for example? He to whom the Eternal Word of God speaks is free from the need to theorize" (1,3). "Vain curiosity often spoils your reading of the bible when, for example, you try to understand or argue over passages in it which you ought simply to read and pass by" (1,5). "Never study in order to appear more wise and learned; it is more profitable for you to root out your vices than to be able to answer difficult questions" (3,43).

Comments like these were written, we must remember, in the late fourteenth century, when scholastic philosophy was going to seed. This was the time, too, when laxity in monastic discipline was already apparent. It seemed that those who were most learned in the Church were doing the least to put into practice the knowledge of divine things which they professed to have. Pride of intellect had won out over the humility of heart needed to submit to God.

None the less, an excess of this sort must not lead us to go to the opposite extreme: to approve blind devotion of any sort, provided only that it be sincere. If overintellectualism is a grave fault in one's religious attitude, too much emphasis on the will is at least equally grave. Sincerity is far from being necessarily equated with truth.

When faith becomes too voluntaristic, it becomes self-centered without giving proper regard to outside facts. The believer who puts all the emphasis on the will to the exclusion of the intellect neglects reason in doing good. Instead, he lays the burden solely on his will. He operates on the principle, "Do it even though you do not know why. Do it, even though it appears contrary to reason, even though you have no rational basis for your action." Thus, the will goes forward blindly without the use of the guiding light of the intellect leading it to adhere to what it should.

It is cold comfort and actually no excuse to claim that if a mistake is being made by reliance exclusively on good will, at least the mistake is "in the right direction." It is still a mistake! The great number of religious revolts led by fanatical reformers, often enough in apparent good will, gives us sufficient evidence how dangerous such ignorance can be. When proponents of voluntarism see the damage wrought by godless learning, they react in this direction and claim that innocence has first rights. They forget, however, that *ignorant* innocence can soon merge easily into stubborn, self-willed revolt.

The testimony of St. Teresa of Avila, the sixteenth century mystic, is appropriate to quote here. Teresa was nothing if not a level-headed woman who showed her many-sided genius in varied talents linked with her high sanctity. On the one hand, she repeatedly complains of the harm done the Church by scholars whose lives did not jibe with their theological learning; but Teresa never subscribes to the thesis that virtue of the will should be cultivated apart from science in the intellect.

In one passage of her *Autobiography* she writes, "I was always fond of learned men, though those confessors who were only half-learned did my soul much harm, because they had not the learning I desired. It is better for directors who are virtuous and full of holy manners to have no learning at all rather than little; because those who have none, will not trust themselves without asking the opinions of others who are learned, and neither could I trust them myself. But I was never deceived by any truly learned men" (Chapter 5).

We note that Teresa wishes spiritual directors to be *neither* religiously tepid *nor* theologically ignorant. Her apparent preference for the holy but ignorant director is expressed only because his holiness will be presumed to see the defects of his ignorance, and he will be humble enough to seek competent advice to make up for this. At the same time, the half-informed man with his dangerous "little knowledge" will be too conceited to admit how much he lacks. Her final judgment compensates for the somewhat disparaging opinions of the *Imitation of Christ*. "*I was never deceived by any truly learned men.*"

Of course, we admit throughout that holiness of will, theoretically considered, is superior to knowledge of intellect. The point we are making is that in the practical order *both* of these qualities ought to be present. The dangers of an unenlightened devotion can appear in forms much more pernicious than the mistakes of the apocryphal legends, as we saw them, in stretching St. Joseph's age. The appeal of the Church to those outside the fold is drastically weakened when the doctrine of the Church is presented as if it had no foundation or confirmation in reason.

In this regard we can recall the deplorable extremes of fideism and traditionalism in the nineteenth century. As devout Catholics saw rationalism apparently sweeping away the foundations of the Faith, they fell back into an isolationist defense and wished to claim that only faith and tradition devoid of an intellectual basis could be relied on. The Vatican Council sharply combated such an approach when in 1870 it made it clear that faith and reason should go hand in hand. In other words, there is no real conflict between voluntarism and intellectualism provided holiness of will is cultivated according to the light of well ordered reason. Any other policy would be an insult to God, who gave us a mind to be filled with proper knowledge as well as a will to be lovingly subjected to its Creator and His laws.

In the practical order, how can a modern follower of Christ obtain such an enlightened attitude? The first and basic principle is to know the Faith, to know why and what one is essentially obligated to believe. This substratum can then be built up by reading and intelligent discussion so as to keep abreast of the growth of knowledge, as far as one's time, talents, and duties of state of life permit. On open questions an open mind is certainly permitted and is not contrary to the thinking of the Church, provided one follows reasonable doctrine and is willing to submit to the Church if ever by its authority it decides the moot points.

Connected with this attitude would be a conservative outlook on claims of private revelations, extraordinary phenomena claiming preternatural origin, extreme penances, and forms of religious devotion that seem to be more showy than solid. In one's private spiritual life the emphasis should be not on obtaining emotional reactions from prayer and good works, but rather on doing such with the intention of pleasing God, no matter how "holy" the individual may or may not "feel." This never means that the action of the will is not cultivated. Instead, the main goal is that the will be developed to seek holiness and perfection *reasonably,* according to proper knowledge.

When such knowledge is not used, religious emotion can be mistaken for true holiness, or false standards are set up incompatible with a particular state of life. The rules of a contemplative order certainly do not hold true in family life. For that matter, not even the rules of an active order would have such value. The *ideals*, of course, would be the same, as ultimate goals; but the means of reaching them are certainly different. St. Thomas Aquinas says in this connection, "Contemplatives may with praise abstain from certain pleasures . . . but those engaged in bodily works and generation of the species may not with praise abstain from these pleasures" (*Summa Theologica*, 2a 2ae, q. 142, art. 1 ad 2).

## Discouragement from Impossible Goals

Our aim throughout should be devotion of the will, enlightened by the intellect. When this goal is forgotten, discouragement can easily occur in the spiritual life. Ignorant attitudes can recur, such as, "I'm a failure spiritually because I have done nothing extraordinary. I am not a mystic, and I don't even want to be, even if I could."

Actually, this is not a single difficulty. It is based on at least a half-dozen misunderstandings and calls for proper information. In its basis it forgets that holiness is proportionate to the love of God, the degree of sanctifying grace in one's soul. Again, the word "mystic" means so many different things to different people. To some it connotes visions, revelations, stigmata; to others, it indicates a life of seraphic prayer during which the subject seems to be suspended between heaven and earth and out of contact, as it were, with the humdrum distractions of everyday life. Still others think of mysticism as identical with a life of terrifying austerity.

The original difficulty goes even further. It falsely supposes, we repeat, that living for God means the emotional perception of some unusual element in one's life. It is often joined, too, with the belief that a less perfect state of life is therefore *im*perfect; and how can spiritual ideals be aimed at when there is no chance to move outside the constricting limits of one's ordinary duties?

Probably the best place to begin in discussing these misunderstandings is to underline the importance of the love of God. This is holiness, and this is the one thing necessary. Holiness means at its roots "to be set apart for God." In other words it is the quality of being Godlike. But since we are creatures with free will, we have the choice of determining how much our own wills are to be conformed to the divine will, the one and only absolute norm and source of good. To subordinate our individual desires to the law of God requires some degree of sacrifice. The generosity with which we give God this sacrifice will indicate the degree in which we love Him.

So often we tend to confuse the love of God as it really should be, with a caricature of the love of God as we think it is. It is certainly not the soft, sweet emotional reaction of having the "feeling" that we love God. The emotions can come or go, sometimes with little or no control on our part. It is true that they may *also* be present *together* with our love of God, but the point is that these feelings do not mean in themselves that the love of God is (or is not) in our heart. We may have them at times when we are denying God the obedience He asks and deserves. On the other hand, they may be absent when our will is wholly devoted to what God wants.

Jesus gave us a reliable answer to this question of determining how much we love God. "If you love Me, observe My commandments" (Jn. 14:15). Our actions, then, are the touchstones of our intentions. They reveal what goes on inside us.

And yet even this very norm of keeping God's commandments can be a source of disquiet for the worried soul. We can fancy a rejoinder put into words something like this. "Yes, Jesus was correct when He said that true love would lead to good actions. That is my own trouble. I look at my actions, and I see so many faults mixed in with them that I am convinced of a lack of love, instead of the love of God that should be there. Would it not show itself more strongly if it were genuinely in my heart?"

The solution here is to distinguish between what is essential and what is not. The essential consists in the avoidance of mortal sin by the proper performance of the duties of our state of life, as dictated by the Commandments and the teachings of the Church. True, to say that this minimum indicates a love of God does not sound very inspiring or very generous. None the less, the fact always remains that this *is* the required minimum, and therefore it does indicate some love of God.

A desire to root out deliberate faults which would endanger this essential minimum represents love at a higher level. Such is the will on our part to keep deliberate venial sin out of our lives and, as far as possible, to reduce semideliberate venial sin as well. Gauged by our Lord's own words, the keeping of His commandments to the extent of avoiding venial sin clearly indicates that a much more generous love exists.

Another question logically occurs at this point. "But if my love of God were actually strong, would I not be completely free from all sin?" The answer to this question is a decided "No, you would not be necessarily free from your faults." There are degrees upon degrees of loving God. We must keep in mind two apparently opposing facts. On the one hand, if we love God, we will avoid serious sin and in general, deliberate venial sin, but unless our love be heroic, it is likely that our faults will remain. On the other hand, this reminder of our weakness keeps us spiritually humble and spurs us on to purify the love already energizing us. We ought not forget the explicit Catholic doctrine concerning venial sin. The Council of Trent defined that the just man cannot avoid all venial sin throughout his entire life without receiving a special privilege of grace from God.

The question here does not ask whether or not we are able to avoid each venial sin, taken individually, for the answer to that is an unqualified "Yes." God gives us the necessary grace. If we have a true will to do so, we can cooperate with this grace and faithfully avoid each venial sin. But how will we have this true will?

The Trent definition refers to a fact well known from daily experience. Repeatedly we find that we have the power to perform individual actions. When we add up these actions, however, new difficulties arise because now a series is to be performed. We get lazy, disgusted, tired, or perhaps our attention is distracted or monotony sets in, all in such a way that somewhere along the line we will fall into a venial sin. God gives us the grace to avoid, so to speak, venial sin #1, #2, #3, #4, etc. Yet even though He is helping us in each individual case, the "strain" of being "so good" catches up with us, so to speak, somewhere along the line. Thus, we need an added extraordinary help from God if we are to commit absolutely no faults during our life.

We have no right whatsoever to such an additional grace. It is, therefore, correct to say that God permits us to fall into venial sin of our own free will. The privilege He has granted on rare occasions has been given to those who already are cooperating with His grace in outstanding fashion. It would seem that even very great saints gave way to semideliberate venial sins, always despite their heroic fidelity to God's will in all other respects.

The existence of this specially rare gift of God does not afford us any excuse for the venial sins which remain in our life. Such faults simply point out a limitation to our generosity which still persists in us. Yet, always in the interests of truth and peace of heart, we *must* insist with ourselves that our venial failings do *not* mean a lack of essential and reasonably generous love of God.

A simple parable can indicate this difference between serious and minor failings, mortal and venial sin. This story seems to have originated with an old missionary teaching catechism to children in one of the earliest parishes in Chicago. Like so many stories first intended for children, it bears an even stronger and clearer moral for the adult.

"Our soul"—so it goes—"is like a little house with doors and windows. The doors and windows are screened and can be locked from the inside. Outside, are the elephants (mortal sin) and the flies (venial sin). The elephants can frighten us as they look into the windows, but not a single one can enter unless we go to the door, hold it wide open, and invite him in.

"On the other hand, the flies will come in despite our best efforts. As we open and close the doors and windows, our half-thinking carelessness will sometimes let some of them slip by for a moment. Even with these accidents, even if our house gets full of flies, all the flies in the world do not equal one elephant.

"But if we are deliberately careless, if we deliberately open the doors to as many flies as possible (since, after all, flies are not elephants), then eventually we will in all likelihood lose our fear of letting in the elephants as well. That is the way we can move from venial sin to mortal sin. All the venial faults in the world do not equal one mortal sin, but habits in giving in to one can lead to actions and even habits in indulging the other."

This little allegory has the benefit of encouraging us on our success in keeping the essential love of God in avoiding mortal sin, and of buttressing this love by staying away from deliberate venial sin as well. It is true that we should always look forward, and we should see how much is lacking still for our perfection, in order to keep ourselves humble; but it seems equally true that we ought to look behind us, to see how much we have gained in our spiritual striving by means of the help of God's grace, in order to keep ourselves encouraged.

### The Question of Perfection

Earlier we mentioned that the "I-can't-be-a-mystic" attitude of inferiority in the spiritual life is often found joined with the belief that a less perfect state of life is therefore imperfect. The belief is, of course, not correct. Only God knows how many souls are crippled with this discouraging conviction. To eliminate it, again we must refer to elementary definitions.

To quote, "Any being is perfect in the natural order when it is finished, completed, hence when it has attained its end. 'Each is said to be perfect in so far as it attains its own end, which is the highest perfection of anything' (Aquinas, *Summa Theologica,* 2a 2ae, q. 184, art. 1). This constitutes *absolute* perfection. However, there is also a *relative* and *progressive* perfection which consists in the approach toward that end by the development of all one's faculties and the carrying out in practice of all duties, in accordance with the dictates of the natural law as manifested by right reason" (A. Tanquerey, *The Spiritual Life,* No. 306).

There can be no doubt that our perfection consists in our love of God and thence in our love of our neighbor. God has given us definite laws—principally, the Ten Commandments—and in addition has invited us to do more than we have been commanded. These invitations are called the counsels, such as voluntary poverty or virginity for Christ's sake. Our perfection, then, will result from our observance of the Commandments and our following at least the spirit of some of the counsels.

Worries needlessly beset souls wishing to serve God when they wonder about their perfection. For example, the married state and the single state of life in the world are called less perfect than the priesthood and/or the religious state. But this description, we must insist, refers only to the state of life as such. It does not refer to the persons in that state, considered each with particular callings from God.

One of the best analyses of this difficulty has been presented by Canon Masure, whose comments we paraphrase here. The problem of degrees of perfection, he says, is a question so hard to answer because it has often been badly formulated, badly expressed, and sometimes is a completely useless query. A Christian may be perfect without being in a state of perfection, and a sinner may be in a state of perfection without being perfect. "The perfection that resides in the love of God consists in placing oneself in the situation that will permit this individual to correspond most completely with the intentions God has for him or for her. This means that the person will seek to accomplish the greatest number of acts of charity of which he or she is personally capable, according to the temperament, heredity, training, and legitimate tastes God has granted."

"We ought to be less concerned with choosing a state of life than with collaborating in the work of creation, of the Incarnation, and the Redemption within the exhaustive limits of our aptitudes, our means, and even of our tastes, not to mention the circumstances amid which we must struggle." The advantage of this attitude is that when we provisionally abstract from the professional framework within which a personal and actual vocation is to be realized (that is, religious life, the priesthood, married life, the single life), the approach tends to pacify worried souls. These are particularly the ones who, first, have no control over their future or even their present; and second, cannot find their way even amid continual changes; and third, hesitate to use extraordinary and very special means, being content to say, "The best place for *me* is where *I* can do the most good."

The way to ask this question, "Where shall I be most perfect?" is to ask where I can best serve, love, and work most efficaciously with God's plan for me. This is anterior and superior to the problem of a choice of a state of life. The state of life chosen causes difficulties for so many. Often it uselessly worries souls eager to be generous. In cases of hesitation or uncertainty, it may inflict painful and hampering inferiority complexes. In brief, we should remember that *the various states of life are states of the love of God;* all are good (Eugene Masure, *Parish Priest,* 94, 95).

Such are some of the lessons we can draw from the fact that our piety should be enlightened, that we should go to God not only with a good will but with a will desirous of finding truth and governing itself according to truth. The legends about the great age of St. Joseph afford an example of how far devotion can go astray in its conclusions when it divorces itself from a rigorous intellectual examination of its motives and its beliefs.

## "It Really Happened"

The study of the age of St. Joseph and the related questions concerning his family background can lead us to still another lesson. That is the lesson of the *reality* of Joseph's life, of his position regarding Mary and Jesus, of the *reality* of Mary, of the *reality* of Jesus. The homely details of everyday life remind us that these events actually took place, even though they occurred almost twenty centuries ago. The "it-really-happened" attitude connected with St. Joseph can extend itself to the Incarnation, as we realize that Jesus appeared on this earth as the God-man and lived among us and gave us an example that we are able to follow.

It has been said that a pilgrim to the Holy Land receives this same impression, "It really happened." As he looks at the hills Jesus saw, as he walks over roads Jesus trod, as he experiences changes of weather Jesus had known, he finds himself deeply moved by the realization that *Jesus lived here.*

The details about Joseph's age and his family background tend to bring about this impression of their reality in us, too. We would make a mistake if we were to limit ourselves to them alone. All the rest of the knowledge we can gain about St. Joseph's life, the information still to come in the following pages, will continue to deepen this conviction, and in the end will help us apply it to Mary and Jesus as well. In such a case Joseph shall have done his task. He shall have given us the best possible gift he could desire for us: closer union with Mary and with Jesus.

# 3.

# St. Joseph's Marriage

"Since the bond of marriage existed between Joseph and the Blessed Virgin, there can be no doubt that more than any other person he approached that supereminent dignity by which the Mother of God is raised far above all created natures."

Pope Leo XIII wrote these words in 1889 in his monumental encyclical on devotion to St. Joseph. He left no doubt as to the sublimity of the union, implying that the dignity of these two holiest of human beings made their marriage unsurpassed among the marriages of all time. "If God gave Joseph as a spouse to the Virgin, He assuredly gave him not only as a companion in life, a witness of her virginity, and the guardian of her honor, but also as a sharer in her exalted dignity by reason of the conjugal tie itself."

Such belief in the genuineness of the marriage of Joseph and our Lady was not always the case. The reasons for doubt and hesitancy are practically the same ones as those which militated against the growth of the devotion to St. Joseph. There was so much need to protect the essentials of the Faith against the predominant heresies in the early Church that little effort was made to study the theoretical nature of a virginal marriage. Far more pressing than this was another factor. If the union described in the gospels were called a genuine marriage, this might imply that Joseph and Mary used their marital rights, to the detriment of the dogma of Mary's virginal motherhood of Jesus.

It does not seem correct to say that one or the other orthodox opinion on the subject was universally adhered to during those first centuries. Instead, Church Fathers often used general phrases that glossed over the idea of a marriage, out of a fear that the genuineness automatically meant the use of marriage rights. The one element they emphasized was that this union was not consummated. With that point made clear, they did not concern themselves further with the technical question whether it was a true marriage or merely had the semblance of one.

In the fourth century St. Augustine was responsible for the first full study of the union, vindicating it as a true marriage, although a few writers before his time had already implied as much. In this approach Augustine set forth the principles which were taken up centuries later by medieval theologians and which resulted in the unanimous Catholic opinion today. The use of the physical rights of marriage was not essential; the spiritual loyalty or contract between the spouses was. None the less, because of the fear of misunderstanding, Joseph and Mary have been called "betrothed" or "espoused" much more frequently than "husband" and "wife."

The word "spouse" is correctly based on the usage in Matthew and Luke. There is, however an important difference in its meaning that is often overlooked or even unknown. Among the Jews of Christ's time the espousal evidently had the force of marriage. It was not considered the promise of future marriage as is our espousal or engagement today. We are not fully aware of all the details of the marriage customs, but this much seems definitely certain.

There were two main ceremonies. The first was called the espousal, and effected a true though incomplete marriage. We argue to this, because various laws of marriage held true for the espoused wife during this time. If her husband died during the year of the espousal, she was called a widow; if she were unfaithful to him, the laws concerning adultery applied to her; if he died childless, the "levirate marriage" custom (mentioned in the previous chapter on page 13) was to be followed.

The espousal normally lasted a year, during which time the espoused husband and wife did not live together. This arrangement originated perhaps out of economic necessity, to allow the head of the household enough time to prepare a home for his wife and future children. We are in doubt concerning the use of marital relations during the year of espousal. On the one hand, it would appear that in some districts the conception or birth of a child from an espoused wife was frowned upon. On the other hand, evidence also exists that if a child was born within the year, the child was considered legitimate provided the husband accepted it as his own.

At the end of the espousal the second ceremony occurred. This solemnized and celebrated the wedding as such. It was a public festive occasion when the bridegroom went to the bride's house accompanied by his party of male friends, to escort her back to his own.

With an understanding of these customs, the references in the gospel begin to fall into their proper places. The Annunciation occurs while our Lady is "a virgin betrothed to a man named Joseph" (Lk. 1:27). Hence, our Lord took human nature in Mary's womb during the year between the espousal and the wedding. The miraculous conception occurred when Mary was already by rights the wife of St. Joseph.

Matthew agrees with Luke. "When Mary His mother had been betrothed to Joseph, before they began to live together, she proved to be with child from the Holy Ghost" (Mt. 1:18). While Joseph was having his ordeal of doubt concerning the source of our Lady's pregnancy and his own obligation by law, the angel appeared to him and said, "Joseph, son of David, fear not to take to thyself Mary thy wife; for what is conceived in her is of the Holy Ghost" (Mt. 1:20). The phrases, "live together" and "take to thyself," evidently refer to the second marriage ceremony, when Joseph would take Mary into his own home and thus publicly acknowledge the Child Jesus as his own, if such acknowledgement were necessary. Need it be added that the Child *was* indeed his own, miraculously given him by God through his virgin wife?

It has been conjectured that the Annunciation happened in the eighth month of the espousal. Two reasons exist for this supposition. From the wording of the gospels, we learn from Luke that Mary visited her cousin Elizabeth for three months. She left for this visit directly after the angel's message had been delivered. Matthew tells us of St. Joseph's doubt, occurring shortly before the wedding. Mary must have returned from her three-month visit shortly before the wedding, for after four months of pregnancy her condition would gradually have become public knowledge. With her own keen sense of justice she would not have been unfair to Joseph, allowing him to go forward with wedding preparations while left in ignorance of her conception.

Precisely how Joseph and our Lady earlier came to know each other for the first time has been a question that has always intrigued writers on the subject. Most likely, some sort of family price arrangement was made between Joseph and Mary's father, according to contemporary custom. The exact way in which divine providence brought about this marriage of all marriages must remain hidden from us until the veils of time are replaced with the full knowledge of eternity.

Less difficult for us is the problem of deducing God's reasons for the union. One of the favorite motivations suggested since the time of early Fathers of the Church was the belief that the devil was to be deceived by the marriage, so that he would not be able to guess its fruit to be divine. Actually, modern opinion inclines to say that God could have prevented the devil from having premature access to the knowledge of our Lord's Incarnation and divinity in ways much more convenient and much more effective than this.

First among the reasons for the marriage seems to have been the fact that God was following His own law. Children are to be conceived, born, received, and reared within the bonds of marriage. Jesus

Christ was to be no exception on this score. The marriage protected our Lady's honor when she bore Jesus. Joseph her husband acted not only as a witness to her perpetual virginity, but also as a trusted friend and protector. We must not forget that Mary was a thoroughly human woman and wife. Despite her unexcelled holiness—or in full accordance with it?—she craved and needed the protection and love of a husband, once God had decreed family life for her. Her marriage also cloaked the mystery of the Incarnation, temporarily hiding the secret of Christ's divine origin until such time as He saw fit to reveal it during His Public Life.

For Jesus as well as for Mary, there was need of protection and love. God certainly planned that our Lord's childhood and growing years were to be within a family circle that was as ordinary as possible. In this environment, unless constant miracles had been worked—which evidently was not the case—Jesus desired and deserved the affection of a father, one who would support Him and teach Him as well, as far as human nature and His experimental human knowledge were concerned. The text of Luke tells us how normal was Christ's youth, how natural His dependence on His parents: "But He went down with them and came to Nazareth, and rendered them submission. . . . And Jesus advanced in wisdom and age, and in grace with God and man" (Lk. 2:51, 52).

Rarely if ever has the subject been discussed, whether the marriage was brought into existence in a subordinate way for St. Joseph's sake as well as for Mary and for Jesus. The reason for this silence is easy to discover. Paramount in the plan of God is the Incarnation; and the marriage was the means God used to introduce Jesus into the world. St. Thomas has phrased the idea succinctly. "The marriage was specially ordained for this purpose, that the Child should be received and brought up within it" (*In IV Sent.*, d. 30, q. 2, a. 2, ad 4).

None the less, while admitting that the purpose of the marriage was essentially oriented toward the service of the Incarnation of our Lord, in all reverence we can discern some purposes in it dealing with St. Joseph. For him the marriage was to be in God's plans the divinely ordained channel to his high holiness. Without it, he would have lacked his superlative relationship to Mary and therefore to Jesus, for Joseph is all that he is, through Mary and because of Mary. The marriage gave him a wife and a son—the two loves that were dearest to God and to St. Joseph on the face of the earth. In a later chapter we shall see the full import of Joseph's fatherly relationship to Jesus. Suffice it here to say that this, too, came to the Saint because of and through his marriage to Mary.

As for Joseph's position with respect to our Lady, we have Leo XIII's summation as our further guide. "Marriage is the closest possible union and relationship whereby each spouse mutually participates in the goods of the other" (*Quamquam Pluries*). This mutual participation between Mary and Joseph was not, of course, exactly equal, for Mary's holiness and dignity are so much greater. None the less, we can gain a proportionate idea of Joseph's sanctity when we reflect that God would hardly choose an unworthy man to be the life partner of our Lady. If any marriage was ever made in heaven, this one certainly was! By it Joseph was made a confidant and closest friend of the Mother of God. By it, too, Joseph and Mary were bound to each other by ties of love that extended to no other human being. Mary would have failed in her duty to her husband had she loved any human person more than him; and Joseph in his turn was bound to devote the heights of his love to her, again as no one else among humans was to receive it.

## The Love of Joseph and Mary

We must not think that because this marriage was made up of the holiest of creatures it was therefore something cold, somber, and forbidding; nor should we fall into the error of supposing that because this marriage was virginal, all affection was rigidly excluded from it. So often this mistake seems to be made, that the use of sex is described as if it were the same as an exchange of affection; and that the observance of chastity, and particularly of perfect chastity, rules out affection. Such a puritanical attitude is inhuman. It tries to deny the fact that love exists in the human heart, and that the human heart craves love in return. It forgets St. John's description, "God is love," (1 Jn. 4:9), and our Lord's own comment, "This is My commandment, that you love one another, as I have loved you" (Jn. 15:12), to quote only two of the many texts of scripture.

Dr. Alphonse Clemens writes, "Few things are more necessary for human well-being than love. It is almost as important as the food we eat or the air we breathe. Physical health, emotional and mental poise, and spiritual progress must have love as a component element of their diet. It is required alike in infancy, childhood, adolescence, adulthood, and old age. The infant deprived of it suffers arrested development; the child without it becomes a twisted personality; the adolescent often turns out delinquent; the adult becomes haggard, embittered, and prematurely old; the aged live out their lives frustrated by disappointment, disillusionment, and loneliness. It is true, even though trite, that 'love makes the world go round'" (*Marriage and the Family*, 48).

The difficulty with us sinful mortals is that only too often we love things or persons that are not good for us, or we love them in a disordered manner. The abuse of love should never lead to its condemnation. Closeness to God does not make human love die out. It rather sanctifies it, lifts it higher, and makes union more close. That is why we are so justified in saying that the love of Joseph and Mary is the most sublime and generous love that ever existed between two human beings, precisely because it was so rooted in and subordinate to their love of God.

Another element of love is its generosity, its sacrificial nature. Love has been defined as the desire to wish well for the beloved, to procure the welfare of the loved one. This characteristic, too, held most true for Mary and Joseph. Each of them lived for the other, in the sense that each wished to help the other serve God better, and no goal can be envisioned higher than this. Mary as the dutiful wife would pray faithfully for her husband. We honor our Lady today as our most powerful mediatrix before the throne of God. If she intercedes for us sinners in so generous a way, how much more earnestly must she not have prayed for Joseph her husband, as she watched him daily wear himself out in her service and that of their divine son? Then, too, her own example added to that of Jesus could have only the effect of inspiring Joseph to greater degrees of generosity and love.

These conditions should not lead us to think that Joseph was, as it were, passively receiving such gifts and doing nothing on his part to merit them. His first selection by God had been made gratuitously, but God foresaw how generously Joseph would cooperate with grace. Thus, while on the one hand God's gifts are bestowed freely, as was this gift of the marriage, none the less, the mysterious workings of free will are taken account of in the divine plan. Joseph's cooperation was no exception.

We might hazard the supposition that if Joseph's marriage to our Lady had never been considered genuine, the Saint's true worth in its turn would never have been discovered and acknowledged. This seems borne out by all historical fact. As long as the legends held sway, wherever their influence extended, Joseph was looked on as a minor character, an accessory in the story of Mary and Jesus who could just as easily be dropped. Such a characterization was thoroughly in line with the legends' denaturing of the marriage. For them the old grandfather Joseph was made a sort of reluctant guardian for Mary (though one can wonder mischievously how the legends failed to perceive that so weak an ancient needed to be taken care of, more than to care for another). There could hardly be any intimate relationship between Joseph and Mary in such a misinterpretation of the gospel texts concerning the marriage.

### The Goodness of Marriage

The marriage of St. Joseph and our Lady is a historical fact having significant consequences. We saw previously that God brought it into existence for grave reasons; it was to serve the Incarnation. Yet we should not stop with an appreciation of its value twenty centuries ago. In many respects it continues to teach its lesson to us today. Most prominent among those lessons are the goodness and the holiness of the married state.

In an earlier age perhaps less was lost when men and women whose vocation did not lie in marriage felt not too much concern for upholding its dignity. We say "perhaps" since one can well debate over the amount of damage done to healthy family life in the past, simply because spouses were not given adequate preparation to enter upon it with a clear vision of its dignity and inherent holiness. We would hardly be fair in saying that Catholic writers and teachers in Church schools taught that marriage was wrong, something evil. In conscience no Catholic could ever approach such heresy. None the less, it does not seem unjust to say that the dignity of marriage was only too often given the minimum of attention. While nothing positive was taught against its being a holy state, some of the teaching concerning the holier states of life in the priesthood and religious life may have left the impression that marriage was tolerated by the Church at best.

In our own day no Catholic, whether living a single life in the world or a religious life dedicated to God, and particularly if in the married state can afford to be indifferent to the defense of Christian marriage. The enemies of marriage are the enemies of God and of God's truth; therefore, they are the enemies of God's people and of their salvation.

The difficulties of the subject again center around the problem of proper emphasis and the avoidance of pernicious extremes. In the one direction of laxity there come to mind all the excesses of modern paganism, which basically denies that God is the third party to every marriage and that God made the laws of marriage. As a result, marriage is debased into a sort of utilitarian contract between man and woman, to be persevered in as long as the parties consider it to their material benefit, their pleasure, or some other selfish advantage. The misuse of sex easily occurs when the first principles governing it are lost sight of.

These errors against marriage quite naturally tend to arouse opposition that counters them sharply. The opposition is not justified to such an extent as to debase the goodness in marriage which God put there. If we were to suggest an oversimplified description of the first extreme as Pelagian, thoroughly independent of God, then similarly the second would be called Manichean or puritanical, rejecting the goodness of God's creation.

The interesting fact is that the second overstrict and highly conservative view of marriage ends up with the same destructive conclusions as does the first, its libertine enemy. Whereas the lawless opinion rules God out of the picture as maker of marriage laws, the second equivalently rules Him out of the picture because marriage and its use of sexual rights become too sordid and vicious.

The truth, of course, lies in between. Marriage, like every creation of God, is good because God made it. Sin can enter only when the creation of God is misused. The partial truth of the first pagan excess is that the use of sex in marriage should not be condemned; the partial truth of the second puritan excess is that the use of sex in marriage should not be left uncontrolled. Any other view insults the goodness of the Creator and the goodness of the universe He made.

This essential goodness which God has put into sex is taught with no mincing of words by St. Thomas. His view reflects throughout the doctrines of the goodness of creation, the purposefulness God built into the universe, and the results of original sin.

"In the state of innocence," Aquinas writes, "nothing [of physical union] happened which was not regulated by reason, not because delight of sense was less, as some say (for instead, sensible pleasure was the greater in proportion to the greater purity of nature and the greater sensibility of the body), but because the power of concupiscence did not throw itself so inordinately into such pleasure. It was curbed by reason, whose place it is not to lessen sensual pleasure but to prevent the force of concupiscence from clinging to it immoderately. By 'immoderately' I mean going beyond the bounds of reason, as a sober person does not take less pleasure in food taken in moderation than does the glutton, but his concupiscence lingers less in such pleasure. . . . God made man and woman before sin. But nothing is void in God's works. Therefore, even if man had not sinned, there would have been physical union, to which the distinction of the sexes is ordained" (*Summa Theologica,* 1, q. 98, art. 2, 2, ad 3; and *sed contra*).

Even a secular periodical has severely criticized the pagan approach to the sacredness of the body and the lack of reverence for creation as God has made it. "If all the indignities that man suffers after he is born were canceled from the books, there would still remain the indignity surrounding the manner of his conception. For the mechanism of conception, the rightful source of his greatest poetry, is a prey to all the smut and ridicule that his simian mind can invent. The mechanism of conception is the mechanism of life, and as such is sacred; yet man has seen fit to suppress it from his speech, hide it from his young, hold it up to shame, smirk at it, peek at it, and vilify it" (*Fortune* magazine, February, 1938, 83).

* * *

We return now to the marriage of Joseph and Mary as a model for every Christian marriage today. It is easy to see that if this is truly a marriage, then it is the sublime exemplar for all marriages and shows forth the basic goodness and opportunities for holiness in this state of life. The difficulty, however, comes to mind over the fact that Joseph's marriage was virginal. How, then, can it be a model for the rank-and-file unions in the world where it is manifestly God's will that parents use their sexual functions to reproduce the human race while symbolizing their spiritual oneness?

Because of this difficulty, a tendency exists in some Catholic circles not to present Mary and Joseph as models for modern couples because they did not use their marital rights. This is an unfortunate error. The essential factor in every marriage is the marriage contract, the mutual giving between husband and wife. The optional bodily symbolism of physical union via the privileges of marriage does not and cannot stand by itself. It has no meaning in itself; it gets its meaning only when it is looked on as an exemplification of a spiritual union that already exists. Here again is where the plan of God enters. The powers of sex may be used by husband and wife to symbolize the perpetual and exclusive union of their wills in marriage. If and when that union is absent, then sex is being perverted outside of the marriage bond, and it becomes a thing of frustration, disgust, and disappointment. A mechanism has been turned against its built-in purpose; all the holiness inherent in its creation has been dragged in the mire of rebellion against the law and loving plan of the Creator.

Thus, it is the *spiritual* union of husband and wife that is critically important in every marriage, giving to the relationship all its subsequent meaning. No couple in the history of the world has ever been linked in so close a union of love and mutual giving as were the virginal husband and wife, Joseph and Mary. In this they serve as the truest leaders for all other spouses of all times.

# 4.
# St. Joseph's Virginity

With regard to virginity, it is imperative that we understand at the outset the constant position of the Church. Following the teaching of St. Paul, who in turn followed our Lord's words, the Church looks on virginity as an optional state of life, a counsel. Marriage is always to be valued as good in itself; virginity taken on for God's sake is better. Earlier, when speaking of vocations we mentioned that the married or virginal states are to be considered more or less perfect only in theory and in the abstract. Concretely, perfection for each individual lies where that person can serve God best with the natural and supernatural gifts at his or her disposal. The important point to keep in mind is that while virginity is more perfect than marriage, this theoretical greater perfection does not imply any *im*perfection or sinfulness in marriage.

The question of St. Joseph's virginity begins, of course, with the further question whether or not the Saint's marriage with our Lady was virginal. If we were to consider the marriage *solely* from the *explicit* testimony in the four gospels, we would not be able to conclude that Joseph and Mary always abstained from the use of their marriage rights. The gospels are absolutely clear in stating that the marriage was virginal before Jesus was born, but they say nothing explicit concerning the virginity of the marriage afterward. Implicitly, however, they lead us to this conclusion, which is confirmed by the unanimous tradition and interpretation of the early Church.

The opening chapters of Matthew and Luke tell us that Jesus was conceived of the Virgin Mary, with no human natural father. They do not enter upon the further question whether other children came to the Holy Family. This does not mean that they suggest such children existed. The implication of the recurring title, "Virgin Mary," is that our Lady's virginity lasted throughout her entire life.

It is pernicious error to read the gospels with an attitude that demands that they answer every question and reveal every detail not even related to their story. They are memoirs of the life of Christ and were never claimed to be complete records. What they assert stands as true as they intended it to be. What they do not assert, may not be rightly alleged as untrue. Opponents of our Lady's perpetual virginity have made a wholly unwarranted use of the argument from silence in this respect.

If any one claims to accept the gospel story, he must accept as a minimum that neither St. Joseph nor any other man was the natural father of Jesus. There has not been too much difficulty on this score. Certain moderns, however, who profess still to be Christians, have resurrected an ancient heresy asserting that Mary had other children by St. Joseph, and that these are the ones whom the gospels call the "brethren of the Lord." This error was first proposed in connection with Matthew 1:25: "And Joseph knew her not till she gave birth to her first-born Son." From this it was claimed that Joseph "knew" Mary after the birth of Jesus, who, being the first-born, was supposedly the first of several children.

The correct meaning is to be sought in the original idiom. Some sixteen centuries ago, St. Jerome demolished the opposite argument when he wrote, "From this passage certain people have perversely conjectured that Mary had other sons, for they assert that he alone is to be called 'first-born' who has brothers. However, it is customary in Holy Scripture to call 'first-born' not him whom brothers follow, but him who is first begotten" (*In Mt.* 1, 25 [ML 26, 25]).

In modern times we have gained striking confirmation of this usage from an archeological find in Egypt. There, a tombstone epitaph of a Jewish bride who died in 5 B.C. reads, "Destiny has led me to the end of my life in the birth-pangs for my first-born son." This mother certainly had no other children, yet her first and only child is called first-born. The title, therefore, had legal implications referring to the rights and obligations of the first son. It no more implied that other children had to follow than our modern use of the word "first aid" must imply hospital care and surgery afterward.

Incidentally, the word "first-born" is not found authentically in Matthew's text (1:25). It is transposed here by a copyist's error from the phrase in Luke 2:7, "She gave birth to her first-born Son." The explanation, however, remains the same, no matter from what part of the gospel we excerpt the words. In the popular mind they are usually accepted as being part of the original of Matthew, and therefore are explained in that context.

Yet another puzzling word exists in Matthew's expression: "Joseph did not know her *till*. . . ." This is a Semitic usage indicating that Joseph was not the natural father of Jesus. In examples of this sort the word "till" designates a state or action up to a certain point but does not necessarily imply a change thereafter. It simply does not discuss whether anything occurred later, limiting itself to the positive statement of fact *up to that point*. One such instance occurs in 2 Kings 6:23: "Michol, the daughter of Saul, had no child until the day of her death." The implication is that she bore no children on that day, and certainly did not do so thereafter. We should not be surprised at such Semitisms in gospel phrases. Our possible desire to have the Bible written in twentieth century English would mean that the book had been and would be proportionately difficult and perhaps unintelligible to people of other races and languages and times.

The difficulty in understanding the "till" sentence correctly was compounded by other gospel references to the "brethren" of Jesus (Mt. 12:46; Jn. 2:12, 7:10). A "Mary the mother of James and Joseph" (Mt. 27:56; Mk. 15:40) was heretically claimed to be also Mary, the mother of Jesus. Again, much of the misunderstanding arose from an ignorance of Semitic idiom. No word for "cousin" or more distant blood relative existed in the Hebrew or Aramaic language. Hence, circumlocutions were used (for example, "son of my brother") or the word "brother" was applied in a wide sense.

Strong evidence exists in the gospels, implying that these "brethren of the Lord" were not children of Joseph and Mary. Mary's words to the angel, "How shall this be, since I know not man?" (Lk. 1:34) have traditionally been accepted in their surface sense, denoting that Mary had at least a serious resolve to remain virginal for the rest of her life, as she evidently had been virginal up to that moment. Again, when Christ was lost in the temple and sought for by Joseph and Mary, the whole context indicates that He was an only child (Lk. 2:41 ff.). The citizens of Nazareth referred to Jesus on one occasion as "the son of Mary" (Mk. 6:3), but nowhere in the gospels are the "brethren" referred to as sons of Mary.

The supercilious attitude revealed by the "brethren" (in Jn. 7:3, 4; Mk. 3:21) suggests that they considered themselves superior to Jesus, hardly, then, younger than he. Otherwise, they would have had no seniority over Him. In such a case they could not have been His uterine brothers because Jesus is so clearly the first-born of Mary.

Finally, when Jesus was dying on the cross, He gave our Lady into the care of St. John the Evangelist (Jn. 19:26, 27). Later in this book we will use this as evidence that St. Joseph had died well before the tragic scene on Calvary occurred. James, Joseph, Simon, and Jude were named in the gospels as among the "brethren" (Mt. 13:55). If they had been blood brothers of Jesus, our Lord would scarcely have entrusted their widowed mother to St. John, who was not even a relative.

Thus, we conclude, although there is theoretically a possible meaning against the virginity of the marriage of Joseph and our Lady, this meaning is not necessary and is absolutely excluded from the sentence, "Joseph knew her not till she gave birth to her first-born Son."

The question logically arises how the virginal marriage of Joseph and our Lady was valid, for the state of virginity seems to exclude the married state. To this the answer can be given that the marriage contract implies a mutual union of wills of husband and wife, together with the granting of rights to each other's body. If neither husband nor wife were to request the physical exercise of these rights, neither would defraud the other, neither would sin against the marriage contract, and the marriage in this fashion would be virginal. The spouses would live as brother and sister.

Such may well be the technical explanation of the fact of this virginal marriage. The reasons for such an arrangement in God's plans are not hard to find. The Second Person of the Blessed Trinity is physically generated from all eternity by God the Father. When that Second Person took on Himself human nature, God did not will to share this natural fatherhood with a human being, even with so holy a man as St. Joseph (although this was not an impossibility). The miraculous origin of Jesus in Mary thus became one of the most powerful proofs of His divinity in the present order of God's providence.

Still another reason comes to mind. The dignity of Mary as the Mother of God was already unsurpassed. It would hardly be fitting that other children issue from the womb that bore such sacred fruit. Throughout, however, the virginal motherhood of our Lady in no way casts any aspersion on the natural plan of reproduction as it normally occurs. Such a supposition would imply that God would derogate from the law He Himself instituted as Creator, and such a contradiction in the divine mind is impossible.

## The Legends and Joseph's Virginity

This rather lengthy consideration of the virginity of the marriage of Joseph and Mary lays down the answer to only one part of the question, "Was St. Joseph himself virginal during his entire life?" We can now assert that Joseph observed perfect chastity during the period of his union with our Lady. What of the time before that? Had Joseph been married previously?

The gospels do not even hint at any answer as to St. Joseph's life-long virginity. A suasive argument, however, exists: Joseph's continence during his marriage might well have been a continuation of his practice in earlier life.

Historically, the apocryphal legends and even some highly reputed Fathers of the Church did not believe in Joseph's virginity. They supported a fiction which claimed that the "brethren" of the Lord were children of Joseph by a former marriage. The reasons behind the claims are evident. Since heretics like Helvidius asserted that the "brethren" were children of Mary and Joseph, well-intentioned Catholics argued to protect the dogma of Mary's virginity by admitting that the "brethren" were indeed related to Jesus, but through St. Joseph. In that case they would have been legal half-brothers of Jesus.

No evidence can be found to support the claim. Those Fathers who advance it do so only using it as an incidental theory and not as absolute fact. Origen, writing in the third century tells us this explicitly. "Induced by the report of the gospel named after Peter or of the Book of James [two of the apocrypha], some affirm that the brethren of Jesus are sons of Joseph from a former wife whom he wedded before Mary. However, those who make this assertion ultimately wish to safeguard the dignity of Mary's virginity in order that the body chosen to minister to the Word . . . might never know man's consortship" (*In Mt.* 10, 17 [MG 13, 875]).

St. Jerome is the stanchest defender of St. Joseph's virginity. In strong protest he writes, "Certain people who follow the ravings of the apocrypha fancy that the brethren of the Lord are sons of Joseph from another wife, and invent a certain woman, Melcha or Escha. As it is contained in the book which we wrote against Helvidius, we understand as brethren of the Lord not the sons of Joseph but the cousins of the Savior, children of Mary [of Clopas, she who was] the Lord's maternal aunt, who is said to be the mother of James the Less and Joseph and Jude. They, as we read, were called brethren of the Lord in another passage of the gospel. Indeed, all scripture indicates that cousins are called brethren" (*In Mt.* 2, 12, 19 [ML 26, 89]).

At this point in our logic the full strength appears of the argument against the great age of St. Joseph. When the legends asserted that Joseph had four sons and two daughters by a previous wife, they created all the more necessity of making Joseph old enough to live in such a marriage. But once the evidence destroys the case for the "old" St. Joseph, the parallel case for Joseph the widower and father of six children is destroyed with it. The reason is simple. If Joseph is young when he marries our Lady at the normal age, sufficient time does not exist for him to become the legendary widower and grandfather.

Thus do we conclude the proof that Joseph like Mary remained virginal for all his life. His virginity would be a sacrifice generously made to God so as to dispose him to cooperate perfectly with the requirements of the vocation to which he was called. Later, we shall see what part his virginity played in giving him an intimate cooperation with the Incarnation of our Lord.

With the apocryphal legends discredited on the two points of St. Joseph's advanced age and supposed earlier marriage, we can logically deny them credence for a third claim they make concerning the Saint: that he was chosen to take charge of the Blessed Virgin by the sign of a miraculously blooming staff. For completeness' sake this tale should be examined point by point in order to separate the possible truth from the certain exaggeration and falsehood.

The *Protoevangel of James* begins by asserting that the high priest in the temple at Jerusalem was told by an angel of the Lord to call together all the widowers "of the people." They were each to bring a staff. A miraculous sign would appear, indicating which of them was to take the Virgin Mary as his wife (apparently in the sense of being only his ward). Joseph with the rest of the men yielded his staff to the high priest, then was the last to receive it from his hands. A dove thereupon came out from the rod and flew upon Joseph's head.

The later enlargement of the legend, the *Gospel of Pseudo-Mat-*

*thew*, presents substantially the same story, with the new detail that the dove emerges from the staff of Joseph and flies off to heaven. A third legend, the *Gospel of the Nativity of Mary*, changes the story still more, adding that the staff buds miraculously, and that a dove comes down from heaven and alights on Joseph's staff.

What is common in all these accounts is the claim that the future husband or guardian of Mary was a widower. We have already pointed out how impossible it was for this designation to be correct, especially since Joseph could not have been old enough. Evidently, however, the legends are eager to show some sort of miraculous selection of Joseph. They select as their pattern the Old Testament miracle of Aaron's blooming staff, related in Numbers 17:1 ff. From our vantage point so many centuries later, we would judge that the chances for a repetition of Aaron's miracle in the case of St. Joseph are very slight indeed. Theoretically it is possible; but did it happen? We can argue only *a priori*, that is, from the nature of events; we have no positive testimony of witnesses. There seems to be only one logical conclusion. If any such striking—and frankly, so garish—a miracle had occurred, the obscurity willed by God for the Incarnation would have been destroyed. Joseph and Mary would have become notorious objects of such wonders and would have remained in the public eye—which is precisely the way the legends continue their tale.

Perhaps the most telling point against the story of the staff is in the claim that Mary was publicly awarded by the high priest to Joseph the widower after she had lived from her third to her fourteenth year in the temple. Here again the legends betray their desire to honor Mary's virginity as much as possible by consigning her to a dwelling-place that is hard to accept. Pious women may indeed have spent much of their time in the Court of Women, beyond which no Jewish woman was permitted to go, but hardly could any young girl have *lived* in the temple as such. One of the legends places Mary's domicile in the very Holy of Holies! Whoever wrote that item for the first time must have been unaware that the Holy of Holies was a relatively small room, bare of all furnishings, and entered only one day in the year by the high priest alone. No other Jewish man, much less a woman or girl, would have been permitted access. The penalty for any such sacrilege was death.

Even less plausible than Mary's living in the temple is the assertion that our Lady was publicly exhibited by the high priest as the virgin to be awarded to the lucky widower. The whole picture is repugnant, far too redolent of a slave on the block. Far from enhancing devotion to our Lady with true honor, the utter impropriety of such an action completely militates against it. We feel grateful that sober logic strongly suggests that no such event took place regarding our Lady. As we mentioned earlier, God's special providence saw to it that Joseph and Mary met each other at the proper time. Precisely how this occurred is a secret into which we cannot and need not delve.

## The Goodness of Virginity

In an age when sexual license is taken for granted and when the faithful Christian must fight against a return to the open licentiousness of ancient paganism, the examples of the virginity of Mary and Joseph take on all the more beauty. Virginity, as practiced by this couple, was not a cold, repelling rejection of sexual pleasure, as if such pleasure were wrong. Instead, virginity meant a special consecration of their love whereby they rose to God more directly than if their love had gone to Him through another created thing, namely, the use of their marriage rights.

Both channels of love are good, virginal love and love symbolized by physical union in marriage. One is more perfect in itself. Each of us has his or her special calling, as St. Paul said so clearly in his letter to the Corinthians (1 Cor. 7:7). No matter what the calling may be, whether it be marriage, the single state in the world, or the religious state consecrated to God, the existence of dedicated virginity inculcates the lesson of the sacredness of the body.

If virginity is looked on in an analogous sense as the reticence whereby one does not give oneself wholly to any other human being but reserves total giving for God alone, then in a certain way all who adhere to God's law have a virginity of soul. The fact that we reject sin and embrace God's will means a policy of reticence and reservation toward created things. When reduced to its ultimate meaning, the promise to obey God's law excludes the gift of one's self to any creature whenever such giving is forbidden. In other words when we do good and avoid evil, we are sacrificing all preferences for things and persons so as to put the Creator first. This same sense of consecration is extended when actual virginity is offered to God.

St. Augustine was second to none in extolling the spiritual benefits of virginity. None the less, he presents an excellent parallel between virginity and marriage, showing how both have their place of honor in the Church. "That the invited Lord came to the wedding [at Cana]," he writes, "shows that He wished to confirm the fact that He Himself had made marriage. For there would be those of whom Paul speaks, prohibiting marriage and saying that marriage was evil and that the devil had created it. But the same Lord says in the gospel when asked whether it was permitted to dismiss a wife for any cause that it was not permitted to dismiss a wife except for fornication. In this reply, if you recall, He says, 'What God has joined, let no man separate.' The well-instructed in the Catholic faith know that God made marriage; and that just as the union or joining is from God, so divorce is from the devil. . . . Nor are those who vow virginity to God, although they hold a rank of greater honor in the Church, without marriage; for even they pertain to marriage, together with the entire Church in the marriage where the spouse is Christ" (*Tract.* 9 *in Ioann.*, 2 [ML 35, 1458]).

Against all the errors of modern times concerning marriage and virginity, Pius XII reaffirmed the traditional truths of the Church in his encyclical, *Holy Virginity.* "This, then, is the primary purpose, this the central idea of Christian virginity: to aim only at the divine, to turn thereto the whole mind and soul; to want to please God in everything, to think of Him continually, to consecrate body and soul completely to Him.

"Souls desirous of a total consecration to the service of God and neighbor embrace the state of virginity [because of] the numerous advantages for advancement in spiritual life which derive from a complete renouncement of all sexual pleasure. It is not to be thought that such pleasure, when it arises from lawful marriage, is reprehensible in itself; on the contrary, the chaste use of marriage is ennobled and sanctified by a special sacrament. . . . Nevertheless, it must be equally admitted that as a consequence of the fall of Adam the lower faculties of human nature are no longer obedient to right reason, and may involve man in dishonorable actions. . . . Persons who desire to consecrate themselves to God's service embrace the state of virginity as a liberation, in order to be more entirely at God's disposition and devoted to the good of their neighbor."

True virginity, the Pope notes, is not motivated by selfish spiritual pride. It "is not a Christian virtue unless we embrace it 'for the kingdom of heaven' (Mt. 19:12); that is, unless we take up this way of life precisely to be able to devote ourselves more freely to divine things to attain heaven more surely, and with skillful efforts to lead others more readily to the kingdom of heaven.

"Those therefore who do not marry because of exaggerated self-interest or . . . because they shun the burdens of marriage, or because like Pharisees they proudly flaunt their physical integrity, an attitude which has been condemned . . . , lest men and women renounce marriage as though it were something despicable instead of because virginity is something beautiful and holy—none of these can claim for themselves the honor of Christian virginity."

To quote Augustine on this score, "Virginity is not honored because it is bodily integrity but because it is something dedicated to God. . . . Nor do we extol virgins because they are virgins, but because they are virgins dedicated to God in loving continence" (*De sancta virg.*, 8, 11 [ML 38, 400]).

The acceptance of voluntary virginity, Pope Pius resumes, must never be looked on as a condemnation of marriage, especially when this is done for the sake of freedom from the solicitude necessary in the married state. "The Apostle [Paul] is not reproving men because they are concerned about their wives, nor does he reprehend wives because they seek to please their husbands; rather is he asserting clearly that their hearts are divided between love of God and love of their spouse, and beset by gnawing cares, and so by reason of the duties of their married state they can hardly be free to contemplate the divine. For the duty of the married life to which they are bound clearly demands, 'They shall be two in one flesh' (Gen. 2:24). For spouses are to be bound to each other by mutual bonds both in joy and in sorrow" (*Holy Virginity*, March 25, 1954, Paulist Press edition, parag. 16, 34, 35, 32, 13, 18, 30, 31).

To summarize the whole body of doctrine on this subject, marriage is holy and good because husbands and wives go through each other to God. Virginity taken on for the love of God is better and more holy in itself because the virginal man and virginal woman go to God more directly, are freed from more earthly cares, and thus can devote themselves more completely to the service of God.

The virginal marriage of Joseph and our Lady is the unique example that can be imitated by all persons, no matter what their state of life.

# 5.
# St. Joseph's Doubt

A poignant episode is connected with St. Joseph's initiation into the secret of the "Word made flesh." As Matthew relates it, "Now, the birth of Jesus Christ was in this wise: When Mary His mother had been betrothed to Joseph, before they began to live together, she proved to be with child from the Holy Ghost. Joseph, her husband, however, being a just man and unwilling to expose her to publicity, was minded to give her a private release; but while he reflected about this, behold, an angel of the Lord appeared to him in a dream-vision, saying: 'Joseph, son of David, fear not to take to thyself Mary thy wife; for what is conceived in her is of the Holy Ghost. And she shall give birth to a Son, and thou shalt call His name Jesus; for He shall save His people from their sins'" (Mt. 1:18–21).

Mary had been gone from her home in Nazareth for more than three months since the time the Angel had told her she was to be the Mother of God. The year of her espousal was evidently drawing to a close. In justice to Joseph, she had to let him know of her pregnancy. At the same time she must have felt that God had not authorized her to reveal its cause. No matter what pain might be inflicted on the man who was closest to her heart, she could only follow her conscience and let God in His providence determine what would happen.

The whole experience with its distressing doubt and worry is usually described as a cross, a source of sorrow, for St. Joseph. May we suggest that our Lady's part in it has been overlooked? It is easy to see the difficulty as far as Joseph was concerned, but we should not stop at this point in an analysis of the misunderstanding. After all, Mary was Joseph's espoused wife, and Mary loved Joseph. These facts can be denied only were we to deny Mary's obedience to the duties of her state of life. God asked a sacrifice of Joseph, but God asked a sacrifice equally of Mary. It was as if He singled out their loyalty to Himself by trying their loyalty to each other. Only after their trial had been successfully braved did He give back to them the gift of each other which He apparently had asked them to sacrifice to Himself.

There is a parallel here with the sacrifice asked of Abraham. First came the many promises to Abraham that God would make him the father of a great nation; then his only son Isaac was conceived and born at a time when only a miracle could have made Abraham's marriage fertile; and finally, God demanded of Abraham to give Isaac back to Him, the son who seemed to be the only means of making the divine promises come true. Abraham passed his test of faith with utter generosity, believing against the evidence of his senses that God would still make him the father of many people even if he no longer had Isaac to carry on his line. Abraham has remained for all time as the symbol of absolute trust in the word of our heavenly Father.

If Abraham's holiness led to such faith on his part, we reasonably conclude how much more faith was exercised by Mary and Joseph. Without making invidious comparisons we are safe in saying that Mary and Joseph represented the apex of holiness attainable by any member of the human race. With such utter sanctity, their love for each other was all the more close because it was free from selfishness. Hence, the sacrifice on their part was all the greater in giving their mutual love back to Him who first bestowed it, and their faith in God throughout was all the more complete.

We are fortunate in our times that biographers of the saints have tried to show the humanness of their subjects, discarding the notion of earlier centuries that the saints should be shown only for edification. That edification only too often meant a censorship on the part of the biographer whereby he deleted from the story of their lives any episode which in his opinion was unworthy of a saint. The supposedly unworthy incidents in their turn did not necessarily reveal weakness, but manifested instead the genuinely human traits of their subjects.

The four evangelists certainly did not belong to the "censorship" school of biography. They tell their four accounts frankly, not concealing in any way incidents that were actually sources of scandal to some. The scandal of the crucifixion heads the list, and beneath it are the frank recitals of Jesus' mental trial in Gethsemane, Peter's triple denial of his master, the apostles' cowardice together with Judas' betrayal, and the petty bickering of the apostles among themselves up to the time of the Last Supper.

In all reverence we can include the story of St. Joseph's doubt with these other narratives of painful reality. The predicament of the two actors, Mary and Joseph, is true to life. Their dilemma is one that spontaneously evokes our sympathy.

It cannot be proved that Joseph was obligated by law to denounce publicly an unfaithful wife. However, any such acceptance of her would have meant a condoning of what appeared to be adultery. If the case was what it seemed to be, the espoused husband would have publicly acknowledged as his own a child who had another father.

The fact of Mary's pregnancy could not be denied. The conjecture has been made that it was not yet publicly noticeable, for our Lady would not have permitted open scandal to reach Joseph's ears by means of public gossip. Therefore, she must have informed him by some means or other before her condition became evident, and before the end of the year of espousal when he was to accept her into his home as his wife.

Some writers have suggested that in accordance with the contemporary customs, the likely procedure in carrying out such a mission was the use of our Lady's mother as the emissary. On the face of it, this hypothesis carries with it a difficulty. If Mary's mother was delegated to tell Joseph of the pregnancy without revealing the cause, how could the mother have done this unless she herself knew of the miraculous conception? If anyone had a right to such knowledge, it was certainly Joseph, the espoused husband, in complete preference over any relative of our Lady. Therefore, to us the logical theory still seems to be the supposition that Mary alone knew the secret, that she felt she was not authorized to divulge it, and that she could only act on her lights by informing Joseph somehow of her pregnancy.

Joseph in his turn was in his own quandary. In the interpretation of his actions three possibilities have been brought forward by scripture commentators in the past. The first opinion holds that Joseph actually thought Mary was guilty of adultery, that he was bound by law to denounce her, and that with a sort of mercy in his heart, he decided to divorce her privately in order to avoid the public shame which would accompany a public divorce. This view is deficient on several counts. If Joseph was certain that Mary had sinned, then he would not have hesitated in his action. The so-called mercy invoked to justify his action would actually have been a violation of the law and a condoning of a sin he knew (or was convinced he knew) had been committed. But—we repeat—*he hesitated,* and this indicates that he felt he did not have evidence of wrongdoing on Mary's part. Arguing from fitness, we would agree that such grave suspicion of grave sin would be most improper for the woman who was the holiest of all God's creatures.

Another interpretation goes to the other extreme in analyzing Joseph's actions. This view holds that Joseph *guessed* that the Messiah had been conceived miraculously in the womb of his espoused wife, and that he wished to put her away because he felt unworthy to be her husband. The opinion has so many weaknesses that it hardly seems necessary to try to enumerate them all. For one thing, how could any ordinary creature, even a man as holy as St. Joseph, ever guess the secret of the Incarnation? Again, why would Joseph have hesitated? Finally, the decision not to go through with the rest of the espousals and to divorce Mary would have been the most uncharitable and gravely culpable injustice Joseph could have perpetrated. Joseph would have been cravenly treating the living ark of the covenant with contempt. His conduct would have been based on cowardly, false humility, not on the sense of true reverence.*

We suggest here what most Church writers in all centuries have adopted as the correct interpretation of St. Joseph's doubt. Joseph simply did not know what to do. On the one hand, he was positively certain that Mary was pregnant. On the other hand, he was not certain that she had committed adultery. Throughout, we should keep in mind that Matthew links Joseph's conduct with the fact that Joseph was a just man. Any action on his part, merciful as it might be, even in the case of private divorce would have exposed

* Another interpretation has been suggested by Father Karl Rahner, S.J., which in its broad outline can be classified as a variant of this opinion. Rahner holds that Mary herself told Joseph that the Child was of the Holy Spirit, and that Joseph in his humility wished to withdraw from the picture, having, as it were, no natural right to remain as the husband of the Mother of God. This is not the place to give long and technical reasons why such a suggestion seems to us to lack solid basis. To put it briefly, the phrase, "Mary proved to be with child from the Holy Ghost" (Mt. 1:18) by no means has to receive the supposedly universal interpretation Rahner claims for it, that Joseph himself discovered Mary's pregnancy. Another assumption that is essential in the Rahner theory is that Mary herself (according to this text) tells Joseph that the Child is of the Holy Spirit. Against this is the fact of the angel's message to Joseph, "Fear not to take to thyself Mary thy wife; for what is conceived in her is of the Holy Ghost" (Mt. 1:20). Rahner can merely claim that this is the angelic confirmation of what Joseph already knew. Finally, while the theory professes to increase the appreciation of Joseph's dignity, it actually ends up by destroying the basis of Joseph's fatherhood. Instead of making Joseph father of Jesus because Jesus is the miraculous fruit of Joseph's marriage, this would make him "father" only extrinsically, that is, because of the command of the angel to take Mary into his home, not because Mary had already been his espoused wife. Rahner seems to disparage the centuries of interpretation following Augustine's analysis, that Joseph is father of Jesus by right of marriage. One wonders, too, how Joseph could have justified casting Mary off, as it were, on her own, by putting her away privately. Such a course of action still appears to us as false humility, unjust to Mary and cowardly, in the face of a supernatural fact. In accordance with a practically unanimous tradition, we believe that the angel's announcement to Joseph was the first indication he had that her pregnancy was miraculous. For a digest of the Rahner theory, cf. *Theology Digest*, 6 (1958), 169 ff.

Mary to publicity to some extent. *Joseph's hesitancy shows us how positive he was that Mary did not and could not sin.* That is why his conduct has been hailed down through all Christian centuries as his absolutely firm witness to the virginity of our Lady, a fact of which he, the closest person on the scene, was firmly convinced.

Once the angel appeared to him and told him that the Child was the Messiah, miraculously conceived, a secondary hesitancy was theoretically possible. How could he acknowledge Jesus as his son since he had not generated Him? The angel practically anticipated this difficulty. The fact that Jesus had been given to Mary, Joseph's espoused wife, meant that Jesus had been thereby given to Joseph. Jesus was Joseph's son in a manner tremendously more sublime than in the case of any other human being. No other fatherhood ever existed for any man on so exalted a level as this.

"Then Joseph, having wakened from sleep, did as the angel of the Lord commanded him, and received his wife" (Mt. 1:24). The wording implies haste. It is easily possible that Joseph celebrated the wedding on the very next day, completing the year of espousal by taking Mary into his home and thereby acknowledging her son as his, too. With this action he began his role of protector of Jesus no less than protector of Mary. Now, initiated into the secret of the ages, he was to carry out his vocation of service, a human holocaust that was completely expendable in the service of Jesus and Mary.

How long Joseph's doubt lasted, we do not know. We suggest that in all likelihood no more than two weeks elapsed between the time of Mary's return from visiting Elizabeth and the appearance of the angel to Joseph. In one sense it was a short period, but in times of mental agony time itself seems to stand still.

The whole incident called for Joseph to give up his love for Mary if need be. The very fact that his conviction of Mary's virtue made him hesitate, thereby made the anguish all the more painful. It was Joseph's Gethsemane. Anyone who can dismiss the whole incident with an indifferent shrug has not penetrated into the closeness that existed between Joseph and Mary. Such a person has not understood how the difficulty of revealing our Lady's miraculous pregnancy threatened a bond of love that was the dearest earthly possession of the two spouses.

Joseph's admirable conduct in this regard has not gone unnoticed. Despite the neglect of the Saint during the early centuries of the Church, in this one connection commentators usually paid tribute to his justice, lavishing on him words of eloquent praise. An unknown author has written, "O inestimable tribute to Mary! Joseph believed in her chastity more than in her womb, in grace more than in nature. He plainly saw the conception, and he was incapable of suspecting adultery. He believed that it was more possible for a woman to conceive without a man than for Mary to be able to sin" (Pseudo-Chrysostom, *Opus Imp. in Matth.*, hom. 1 [MG 56, 632]).

St. Jerome, too, was equally discerning. "This is evidence for Mary, that Joseph, knowing Mary's chastity and wondering at what had occurred, concealed in silence the mystery he did not fathom" (*In Mt.* 1, 2 [ML 26, 24]).

One of the lessons connected with Joseph's doubt is the lesson of faith in God's providence and love, as we have already noted. Also related to it is the fact that God does not spare those He loves, no matter how close they be to Him, no matter how faithful. Joseph and Mary were not exempted from the possibility of grave misunderstanding, and God did not work His miracle at once to spare their feelings.

This does not mean, of course, that God is harsh and unfeeling. In accord with the fact of His loving providence for us, we can discern even from our limited vantage point that the doubt of St. Joseph had true value in witnessing to the virginal conception in our Lady. If Joseph had not been subjected to the trial in the way it happened, such added proof for us would have been lacking.

From the viewpoint of merit for Joseph and Mary, the trial can be looked on as another one in the series of their actions whereby the couple cooperated so perfectly with God's will and offered their actions in union with the redemptive action of Jesus to save the human race. If we had been able to ask them their sentiments at the time of the trial, they would have assured us of their single great desire: to be conformed to God's will as perfectly as possible, in every detail.

### Scrupulosity and Guilt

Joseph's hesitancy involved a mental difficulty before what seemed to be an insuperable obstacle. There, too, a series of lessons unfolds for us, because in our own cases mental hesitancy appears in the face of apparently grave obstacles, nagging, destroying peace of mind, suggesting that God has abandoned us. We call these doubts scruples. Certainly, Joseph's quandary was not a scruple, but the difficulty of his making a choice in such circumstances is related to the difficulties in scrupulous doubts, together with their tendency to ruin proper perspective and mental peace.

So many authors have written so much concerning scruples, their cause and their cure, that one can wonder whether more can profitably be added. Despite the wealth of material already available, there are advantages in presenting still another discussion here. If for no other reason, these are ideas concerning which people should be aware; they deserve further propagation.

What of the individuals who claim they never had a scruple and probably never will have one? They will act prudently if they hold themselves back from an overconfident attitude. Scrupulosity can attack any one at any time of life without warning. Moreover, knowledge of scrupulosity and how painful the malady can be will help toward a kind attitude regarding the scrupulous. Christian charity would be utterly lacking in those who would look down with haughty contempt on persons who are scrupulous, for they are usually so through no deliberate fault of their own.

Exactly what is a scruple? The word is derived from the Latin *scrupulus*, meaning a small pebble or jagged bit of rock. The ancient Romans themselves extended the word to include a harassing doubt.

Today the word is used in varying meanings. We are not using it, of course, in the popular reference to a carefully worked out action or attitude, such as the "scrupulous neatness" of a well dressed man or woman. Instead, in the technical sense we are understanding it here as a vain fear of sin, aroused by groundless apprehension. Linked with this is the inability to make a definite decision in matters of conscience. One is habitually "on the fence," fearing both to do or not to do some action.

These two elements of a scruple pertain to the religious or moral sphere. The parallel fears or inability to make decisions can show up in nonreligious matters as well, as, for instance, in a worry whether doors have been locked, switches and valves turned off, letters inserted into their properly addressed envelopes. This can be a cause of much consolation for a person tormented with religious scruples, to realize that such a state of mental worry appears in secular matters as well. It gives all the more assurance that a religious scruple is not necessarily a sin. It indicates that such doubts can result from a sort of warped mental outlook which has attached itself in this case to things religious instead of things mundane.

Psychiatrists and psychologists have pointed out that scrupulosity is a religious neurosis, rooted in a sense of spiritual insecurity. Hence, the doubts and fears arising from this insecurity drive their subject to follow a supersafe line of conduct. Such a course of action is not possible for humans to observe because human behavior is based on what is called moral certainty, namely, the general, over-all certitude gained by a judgment of how humans normally react. The scrupulous person, however, wishes to have absolute or metaphysical certainty—the "$2 + 2 = 4$" reasoning which represents a standard fantastically impossible to attain in making moral judgments.

The scrupulous person confuses elementary notions of sin. For him, mortal sin exists everywhere. His outlook is predominantly puritanical. Consistent with this want of proportion, he judges that if a thing is wrong, it must always be wrong. There is no gradation in his mind between mortal sin, venial sin, imperfection, and lesser grades of perfection. Usually everything is presumed sinful until and unless it is proved good; pleasure is also presumed to be wrong.

Throughout this description of scrupulosity we must remember that genuine moral doubts arising from ignorance are not genuine scruples. The scruple carries with itself a sense of *habitual* guilt, usually unjustified. This "feeling guilty" may continue long after the moral fault (whether real or imaginary) has been remedied.

Many people are greatly surprised to learn that this sense of guilt is not necessarily correct or desirable. They are even more astounded at the knowledge of the great distinction existing between real guilt, and imaginary or "neurotic" guilt, of the type that underlies scrupulosity.

Real guilt follows upon evil that has actually been done; true remorse is based on real guilt. Imaginary guilt, however, can occur after actions that are only thought to be evil, when in fact no evil has occurred. Imaginary guilt can also accompany real guilt, so that after a sin has been atoned for by sorrow and penance, the exaggerated guilt feeling persists.

The distinguishing mark between real and imaginary guilt is its intellectual or nonintellectual content. In the first case the person has an essentially rational and even cool understanding of the evil done and of the need for penance. In imaginary guilt its bundle of feelings is closely tied in with emotion. Real guilt can be atoned for by acts of penance, and then peace of mind returns. Imaginary guilt, however, is insatiable for expiation. In fact, the more atonement is performed, so much the stronger becomes the impulse to do penance and to make further atonement.

Throughout, real guilt recognizes a proportion between the evil action and the apprehension of guilt because of it. In imaginary guilt this proportion is entirely lacking. One of the telltale signs appears most prominently in this characteristic of "weighing down" its subject. For example, a sharp word is uttered, or perhaps merely a careless noncommittal greeting exchanged; yet the scrupulous person can have from this experience a series of guilt feelings as grave as if he or she had physically beaten to death a helpless and innocent cripple.

Even when evil has been done, imaginary guilt can accompany real guilt. Then, of course, the sense of wrong is out of proportion and far oversteps the malice of the blameworthy action. To complicate the picture still more, real guilt comes after actions which the person consciously recognizes. Imaginary guilt, however, can arise out of repressed drives long forgotten where the cause is no longer consciously known.

Finally, real guilt is independent of bodily states, but imaginary guilt feelings are likely to be linked with states of hunger, fatigue, poor health, repeated frustration, and other failure experiences. True conscience works only with regard to real guilt. Imitation guilt feelings are so overloaded with emotion that they should never be considered the voice of conscience.

What can be offered as a cure for scrupulosity? Certainly, no one answer exists. It has been wisely suggested that scrupulous persons will be able to control scruples once they are convinced that the tendency to be scrupulous will stay in their temperament forever. This does not mean giving in to scruples. Instead, it is the realistic attitude of living with a frame of mind, not so much yielding *to* it, but yielding *before* it, in the sense that a wise retreat can be equivalent to a full-scale advance. Compromises and adjustments are therefore to be made according to the weaknesses of will and judgment which scrupulosity reveals. In this way, wholesale discouragement is avoided because the individual does not look forward to a day when scruples will be gone forever. Perhaps they will be, perhaps they will not. But no matter what the future outcome, this realistic acceptance of the situation relieves tension and fear. One lives now with something tangible, accepted as actual; one does not live with something vague, causing a dread of the unknown.

A parallel of this attitude we are recommending is found in the case of the physically handicapped. Once an invalid accepts the limitation of paralysis, blindness, or a lifetime confined to bed, then he or she is much better able to cope with the problem. As long as the fact is being denied, so it seems, it cannot be met face to face and accepted with peace of mind. We are suggesting the attitude, therefore, that there is no absolute *cure* for scruples, strictly speaking. They can, however, be brought under control and kept under control.

This attitude should be further developed to emphasize a deep, trusting love of God, no matter what one's emotional worries may say. The basic principle is that religion consists in loving God, and servile, mistrusting fear has no place in the mind or heart of those who love Him. If our love of God is so weak that we cannot believe in His mercy for us, we are paying Him no compliment. We should be fully convinced that His goodness far, far overshadows our little efforts.

Accordingly, we should try to develop with equal conviction the deep belief that God, who loves us, loves us as individuals and cares for us. He is not a hard Simon Legree, demanding the impossible and trying to trap us into sinning. He expects us to do our *reasonable* best. He does *not* expect us to be constantly straining with every taut fiber of our being, because such an attitude is hardly the reasonable condition of the normal human being as God has made us.

Scrupulosity means that we are trusting to our own power too much in trying to avoid sin. We are, as it were, trying to lift ourselves up to heaven by means of our own bootstraps. Our emphasis ultimately is too much on "What am *I* doing to make *myself* holy?" instead of, "What am I doing to carry out what *God* wants in my life, *the way He wants it—knowing my limitations, my weaknesses, and my sins?*" We certainly do not serve God best by attempting to set up norms for our own conduct which are not the norms He wishes.

One of the tendencies of the scrupulous person is to attempt to mathematize the spiritual life. We mean by that the habit of counting each and every action and thought and word, down to the smallest details. Again, this is not the way God made human nature. Many of our deeds can be gauged by only a moral estimate, a general-survey judgment, hardly an arithmetical sum. The attitude of complete confidence in God and abandonment of ourselves to Him is the only reasonable spiritual attitude.

Every decision requires energy, and the prolonged indecisiveness resulting from scrupulosity paves the way to more mental fatigue and therefore more mental difficulty in making future decisions on moral matters. This is why the scrupulous person should not argue at great length on what judgment to make. If it is not immediately clear what should be done in a given situation, then the individual should imagine what advice he or she would give to another person in the same predicament.

This is one of the best methods of reaching an objective judgment in a cause touching ourselves. For some reason or other, when we look on ourselves as if we were someone else, we lose the excess of concern for our own welfare that so often can paralyze our thinking. Then, with a relaxed attitude because of confidence in the judgment —made, of course, "as if" for someone else—we can calmly take up our duties again.

In summary, the scrupulous person needs a firm belief in the truth of a reasonably formed conscience, and then the strength to go ahead and do what conscience dictates, without going back on past decisions. One does not argue with scruples. The only answer they are to be given is a firm "no," and this answer should be given after one has done what other reasonable persons would do in similar circumstances. On the other hand, if their imperious demands are heeded, they will only continue to be ever more imperious tyrants.

## Discouragement Again—and Always?

Scrupulosity is often found closely interconnected with an attitude of chronic discouragement, because discouragement can lead to scrupulosity, and prolonged scrupulosity certainly causes discouragement. For this reason, and because discouragement is such an extremely common experience, we have good reason to see what can be done about it.

It has been said—and apparently rightly so—that discouragement is the greatest obstacle for the ordinary person who wants to serve God. The fact that it recurs so often does not seem to help us develop defenses against it. Each time we are discouraged, we tend to forget all the stimulating successes of the past, and to look forward to the future with trepidation and foreboding.

Precisely what do we mean by saying we are discouraged? The word itself comes from the Latin *cor,* "heart," and literally means "losing heart." Informally, we might describe ourselves as being "down," desolate, disgusted, lacking interest in our life, our work, our friends. Our outlook becomes thoroughly pessimistic. All bright hopes seem to vanish as far as we are concerned. In other words, we are discouraged.

In a human way of speaking we should never think of discouragement as directly sent by God. Because it takes away our peace of heart and hinders our service of Him, it cannot be willed by Him as such. However, we should not hesitate in looking on it as a trial of our fidelity. It is permitted by a loving providence like all the other trials of this life to draw us closer to God and to add to the divine glory by helping save souls—our own souls, and others, too. Ultimately, we must never forget that God permits every trial to come to us only for our greater good.

In theory we can consider the devil as causing us to become discouraged, but in the practical order it would not be prudent to consider each and every bout as personally mailed to our address by "his diabolical highness." The reason for this is that we do not understand exactly how the devil works. The fact that his perverted angelic powers are arrayed against us is beyond all doubt, but how and when he uses them is something we do not know with certainty. We are safe in concluding that the devil will make use of discouragement against us when open temptation will not otherwise succeed.

Discouragement normally results directly from our mental and physical state. Knowing how our bodies and our moods react upon us will help soften its effects. None the less, our own experience and the unanimous advice of all experts in the field tell us that we will never conquer discouragement completely. It has been with us in the past, it may perhaps be oppressing us now, and it certainly will be with us in the future. "Forewarned is forearmed" holds true here.

The knowledge of the possible sources of discouragement and the typical way in which we react to them has other advantages, too. The proverb, "Misery loves company," means in this case that we realize that we are not alone in the ups and downs we experience. Not that we rejoice because others have difficulties! Instead, our consolation and strength grows out of the fact that other men and women have weathered the same storms and even worse than we find in our own everyday existence. Their experiences were painful as are ours, but the important fact is that they withstood them. They bore with them for the while, eventually triumphed over them, and even produced works of great value despite—or perhaps because of—the obstacles they met.

A principle that has been used successfully and effectively for thousands of people should work successfully for you, too. This is the realization that discouragement (like our fears) is painful but not necessarily dangerous. Most of our fears about being discouraged are not so much the fears themselves. *The trouble lies in our fear of what these fears will do.* Once we can live our lives with a constant self-reminder that our discouragement will be more or less painful but that it is not of itself dangerous, it will tend to be less deep, of shorter duration, and even less painful.

It is very easy, of course, to set down on paper a list of rules to follow during the periods of discouragement. The discouragement will usually prevent them from taking effect. This has been called the "Yes, but . . ." attitude. None the less, such rules help to form a constructive framework during moments when we are feeling confident of ourselves. In that way they can give strength to "hold on tight" when once the depressing moods have returned.

Always first on any list must come the conviction that discouragement *will* recur, and that when it does, we must believe with as much firmness as possible that it will eventually disappear.

Again, the physical condition of the body will play a great part. Times of sickness or even of fatigue, hunger, and sleepiness normally predispose us to become discouraged. Sometimes a change of diet or the addition of an inexpensive and harmless vitamin supplement (primarily the Vitamin B Complex) is all that is needed to relieve chronic discouragement. The reason is that a food substance of this sort can provide the energy which is needed to make constant daily decisions in meeting constant daily problems.

Man, however, is always soul as well as body. The physical does not account for everything. Hence, mental outlook can influence discouragement also. On the one hand, some sort of stress is good for us, and a certain amount of tension keeps us alert, progressive, achieving. The opposite extremes, however, of too much or too little stress will contribute to a set of discouraging moods.

One case might be that of the man or woman with overambitious ideals. An ideal of this type should be of course accepted as something beyond our reach. When it becomes fantastically out of range, so that no progress can be discerned in approaching it, then it has lost its attractiveness and had better be discarded.

The consciousness of making progress, or of gaining achievement, seems to be the opposite of being discouraged. The sense of achievement leads us to a sense of personal value; hence, the need and desirability of cultivating it. Hence, too, discouragement will find fertile soil in the life of the person who has nothing to do, nothing constructive to accomplish, or no obstacles to overcome. Yet even here there must ever be moderation. Too much to do or too many obstacles to overcome will be a hindrance and will weaken the spirit. It is interesting to note that the *fact* of conquering obstacles does not seem to influence discouragement. It is rather the *realization* of success, whether justified or even not justified, that has effect.

Discouraging situations influence each person more or less strongly, but in general the following cases with religious or moral elements in them are occasions for losing heart.

There might be, first of all, the success of someone else, either spiritually, intellectually, or socially. In such a case we think we must imitate others in every detail, forgetting that each one of us as an individual is different, and therefore can never be copied exactly, nor for that matter, surpassed in exactly the same way. Discouragement here can grow out of a misplaced spiritual ideal, or at a lower level, from a sort of spiritual jealousy.

This is the place to mention the related case of reading lives of austere saints. Sometimes the biographer has exaggerated the marks of supposed holiness to an extent humanly impossible to imitate. Sometimes, too, the austere saints lack an appealing warmth of character. Discouragement can then come easily to the person who reads of their deeds and is repelled rather than attracted.

If we cannot easily make the compensation of seeing how we can imitate the saints in our own state of life, then we should either not read such books that bother us or else deliberately train ourselves to say, "There I can copy, there I can only admire, there perhaps the saint himself was wrong, as so many of them have later admitted."

Even advanced holiness does not necessarily mean perfection of judgment. The saints themselves had their arguments. St. Philip Neri and St. Charles Borromeo clashed hotly over the question of how many priests were to be assigned to do certain work. Peter Canisius feared that Charles Borromeo's strictness would alienate the gentle Swiss. Peter Celestine made countless administrative errors during the few months he reluctantly acted as Pope. In the lives of all the saints we ought to select the elements of heroic generosity which they showed forth. The way in which they applied their principles to everyday life may not always have brought their own prudent approval in later days, but their mistakes were made in good will.

The final point to remember here is that what the saints decided for themselves was *only* for themselves. Every other person can only *apply* the saints' examples to individual needs, talents, and situations.

Still another source of religious discouragement comes from our failings in small things. When such semideliberate selfishness occurs, we seem to be unable to face up to the fact that we have never given ourselves to God completely, and that selfishness remains in us always to some degree. The task of removing it is lifelong. The remedy for the discouragement because of it is to look to the great truths of the Faith.

We should not cripple ourselves, flying away from Jesus with a cry of false humility, "Depart from me, I am a sinner." St. Peter first said these words, but he did not leave Jesus.

Instead of the negative attitude of looking only at our defects, we should emphasize loving God positively. Patience and gradual growth in virtue will weed out some of the selfishness in us. For the rest, we should be grateful that God has given us the grace to be aware of our failings. The knowledge of our own limitations makes us turn to Christ with all the more confidence. Our religious service then becomes more properly centered on God, with less danger of selfish spiritual gratification because of our supposed virtue.

Were Joseph and Mary ever discouraged? We have so little told us of their words that we cannot offer proof in one direction or the other. Certainly, one might conjecture at first thought that their exalted holiness would permit no such weakness. Other indirect evidence, however, exists. In the case of Jesus, the most perfect human nature was assumed by a divine person. Yet Jesus, giving us the height of good example, showed discouragement at certain times in His public life. Our greatest intimate revelation of what went on in our Lord's heart occurred in His agony in Gethsemane.

Jesus was unable to commit sin and could not even have positive imperfection in His life. He did assume the limitations of human nature. Our conclusion must be, then, that discouragement in our feelings is as such neither sinful nor imperfect. If Jesus Himself permitted us to learn that He became disheartened, we are justified in believing that Mary and Joseph, too, had the same cross and difficulty. For us, such knowledge does not make them less approachable or less respected. Instead, their holiness draws us on all the more as we see all the more the problems they had to meet.

# 6.
# St. Joseph's Fatherhood

It is unfortunate that so much of the legendary picture of the first Christmas has become the popular picture. In the popular mind a Roman census is announced. Joseph and Mary saddle a donkey and immediately take the road for Bethlehem. When they arrive there, the town is overflowing with visitors. They go to an inn, only to be rejected by a greedy innkeeper whose price they cannot pay. Mary tells Joseph her time has come, and in a last-minute desperate effort Joseph finds a stable where Mary bears Jesus. Utter poverty surrounds the Child's unexpected birth to such an extent that Mary has to make use of some old rags found in the stable, and these are the swaddling-clothes which wrap the Child; adequate preparations for Him evidently were never made. The shepherds visit the cave within a few moments, bringing their lambs with them as they trudge over the snow-covered ground in the bitterly cold night. Shortly after the shepherds leave, the camels of three Oriental kings come into sight, as a brilliant star precedes them and finally shines down on the infant Jesus in His crib.

So many elements of this impression are doubtful and even erroneous that we will not take the time here to refute them one by one. Instead, a summary of the evidence we can gather concerning the first Christmas and Joseph's part in it will serve to rectify the story.

To begin with, the gospels do not hint in any way that Joseph and Mary remained in Nazareth after their wedding, or that they went directly to Bethlehem on the night of Christ's birth. It is not unlikely that when Joseph was informed of our Lady's miraculous conception, he took her out of Nazareth as soon as possible, perhaps directly after the wedding. There was too much danger that some part of the secret of the Incarnation might accidentally be made manifest, with consequent danger to the reputation and honor of both Mary and Jesus. We know from archeological records that the only Roman census at this period was proclaimed in 8 B.C. in the part of the ancient empire that is now Turkey. Such a proclamation would not necessarily be made in Palestine at the same time, nor would there be an immediacy of obeying it as if the records had to be taken within a week or month. In this respect it has been suggested that St. Joseph used the census as the pretext for taking Mary out of Nazareth.

The trip to Bethlehem was almost ninety miles long from Nazareth in the north of Palestine. Four days would be needed to traverse the route, with Mary riding the donkey and Joseph walking ahead. We are quite certain that Jesus was not born directly upon the arrival in Bethlehem. Perhaps the strongest argument for this view is the logic of St. Joseph's position. The man whom God chose to be the husband of the Virgin Mary and the father of Jesus on earth would hardly have subjected his wife to a ninety-mile journey for four days when she was practically at term. Such a course of conduct would have been unfair to her, and would have endangered the welfare of her unborn divine Child. Joseph was bound by his position to use every reasonable natural means in protecting Jesus and our Lady. He would certainly not presume on God's providence in expecting miracles to be worked in order to undo or prevent the results of his own carelessness or lack of foresight. Mary, too, simply could not have been so unworthy a mother as to risk such a journey at such a time.

Our conclusion, then, is that the couple were at Bethlehem for at least two weeks before Jesus was born. This is confirmed by the wording of St. Luke's gospel which in its original Greek implies, "while they were *still* there," her time for delivery arrived (Lk. 2:6). The gospel in no way says that this occurred immediately after or when they reached their destination.

The mention of swaddling-clothes is another indication that Mary was ready for the Child, and was anything but unprepared. These were the customary bands with which the newborn babes were first covered. Usually, there was a large blanketlike cloth enveloping the child except for his head. Two tight bands further encircled his body at the chest and at the knees, so that he could be carried by another band connecting these two much on the style of the handle of a modern valise.

The popular idea taken from medieval legends that Joseph and Mary were turned away by a hard-hearted innkeeper is completely at variance with the customs of the time and certainly finds no support in Luke's wording. There we are merely told that Mary "laid Him in a manger, because there was no room for them in the inn" (Lk. 2:7). The manger is a food-trough for animals, and the mention of it implicitly tells us that Jesus was born in a place where animals were kept. The inn, especially in so small a hamlet as Bethlehem, was nothing but a stockade with open alcoves around its inside walls and a sturdy gate to keep out robbers at night. To bear the Child amid such surroundings was most unseemly. The filth, the constant bickering, and the lack of privacy were weighty reasons why Joseph would seek shelter for Mary elsewhere. Scripture commentators call particular attention to Luke's phrase, "no room *for them,*" not simply "no room." The whole expression aptly serves as a delicate way to give the reason for the location of Christ's birthplace.

The gospel clearly tells us that an announcement of angels to shepherds in the vicinity brought these men to the feet of the newborn Savior. Since this occurred while they were "keeping the night-vigils over their flock," we suspect that the season was the lambing season, springtime. Only then would it have been logical for shepherds to have watched through the night to give help to their ewes during birth.

The existence of a "white Christmas" is all the more excluded, therefore, not only from the probable springtime date but also from the fact that snow falls rarely in Palestine. Our December 25 date for Christmas was set only after some three hundred years of the Christian era had elapsed. Even then it was intended to substitute for the pagan feast of midwinter; it was not to mark the exact day of Jesus' birth.

As for the coming of the Magi and the misnamed "Christmas star," we shall discuss this in a later chapter. Suffice it here to say that the Magi could not have arrived until at least forty days had elapsed after Christ's birth. The reason is that Jesus was circumcised eight days after He was born, and was presented in the temple at Jerusalem thirty-two days later, to fill out the forty-day interval prescribed by the Law for Mary's purification. On the other hand, the Holy Family was forced to flee into Egypt directly after the Magi's visit. Hence, the Magi, we know, did not reach Bethlehem until after the circumcision and presentation of Jesus had occurred, and that was well after the day on which Jesus was born.

With the birth of Jesus, the tableau of the Holy Family is complete: Jesus the son, Mary the mother, and Joseph as the father. We have already looked at St. Joseph in his position as virginal husband of Mary; we can reverently ask now how he is to be considered the father of Jesus.

## Joseph's Fatherly Titles

The gospels of Matthew and Luke in their first two chapters make it crystal clear that Joseph did not generate Jesus. None the less, the texts which directly concern St. Joseph show that he is father of Jesus in some unique sense that is not physical. He is listed in the genealogies (of Mt. 1 and Lk. 3) as one of the legal ancestors of

Jesus. He is given parental and therefore paternal authority: "Thou shalt call His Name Jesus. . . . he called His Name Jesus" (Mt. 1:21, 25). Joseph governs both Jesus and Mary: "So [Joseph] rose and took the Child and His mother by night and retired to Egypt. . . . So he arose, and took the Child and His mother and went to the land of Israel. . . . he retired to the region of Galilee. And he went and settled in a town called Nazareth" (Mt. 2:14, 22, 23). Joseph in all these cases makes the decisions as head of the household.

This authority was earlier recognized when the angel appeared in a dream to warn him to flee into Egypt. It is explicitly stated again when Jesus "went down with *them* and came to Nazareth, and rendered *them* submission" (Lk. 2:51). Not only do the people of Nazareth refer to St. Joseph as the father of Jesus—"Is not this Jesus the son of Joseph, whose father and mother we know?" (Jn. 6:42)—but Mary herself calls Joseph "father" and Luke refers to Joseph on a parallel with Mary as a "parent." "The parents brought in the child Jesus" (Lk. 2:27). "His father and mother were filled with admiration at the things that were spoken about Him" (Lk. 2:33). "His parents went every year to Jerusalem at the feast of the Passover" (Lk. 2:41). "His mother said to Him, 'My Child, why hast Thou treated us so? Indeed, Thy father and I have been searching for Thee in great distress!'" (Lk. 2:48).

If Luke alone had used the title "parent," we might theoretically claim that he was following common opinion, contrary to his knowledge that Joseph was not the natural father of Jesus. However, when Mary is the one who calls Joseph "father," there is no possibility that she is using an otiose title for the sake of the bystanders. She knew better than any other human that Joseph did not generate her divine Son, yet she did not hesitate to link his fatherly position with her own genuine motherhood in a moment of deep sorrow. The conclusion must be that in some sense or other, St. Joseph is truly the father of Jesus although not the natural father.

In 1912 Cardinal Billot wrote a trenchant analysis of the difficulty in describing St. Joseph's fatherhood. "Since this instance is in every way unique, no name exists in the human vocabulary by which it can be indicated. That is why we are able to say what title should not be given Joseph more easily than we can say what title should be used" (*De Verbo Incarnato*, 421).

The solution to the problem depends on what is meant by the word "father." Normally, it is used to indicate that a man has generated a son or daughter. However, the full meaning of fatherhood in human beings does not stop with generation. In animals there is little or no permanent effect outside of the fact that a new individual has been brought into existence. In human beings, however, just because we have an intellect and a will and therefore we can know and love, the father has an obligation to continue the work he began, namely, to support, educate, and love the child whom he brought into existence from his wife. This continuation of generation, as it were, makes up the moral bond of fatherhood, a spiritual bond that exists between father and child. It is so important because this is actually the distinguishing element that makes human fatherhood different from that of brute animals. There is no "love" of a stallion for the colt it has generated.

Sometimes it happens that this moral bond has existed between a man and a child in cases where the father has not generated the son. Such would be instances where a child is adopted by a guardian and is accepted and lovingly reared by his adoptive father. We should notice in cases of adoptive fatherhood of this sort that although generation has not occurred, the characteristic that is distinctive of human fatherhood is present: the bond of love between father and son.

We can now apply these ideas to St. Joseph. In the first place Joseph did not generate Jesus. Therefore he cannot be called the *natural* father of our Lord. Since Jesus is the Second Person of the Blessed Trinity, only the Eternal Father, God the Father, already generates Him according to the mystery of three Persons in one God.

This does not mean that we should say Joseph is the adoptive father of Jesus on earth. Such an answer might seem to be correct at first sight, according to our earlier explanation of fatherhood, for Joseph did not generate Jesus. Moreover, he did accept Him as his Son, according to a relationship of fatherly love and rearing. None the less, strictly and correctly speaking, Joseph should not be called the "adoptive father of Jesus."

The reason is that an adopted child is alien to the family which adopts him. He was brought into the world by other parents than the ones who adopted him. In the case of Jesus this is not what happened. God expressly brought the Holy Family of Joseph and Mary into existence so that Jesus could be brought into the world within this family, and could be reared, educated, and loved there. Jesus was miraculously conceived and born of the Blessed Virgin when she was already Joseph's wife. By the bonds of marriage any children she had within her marriage belonged to Joseph her husband. The normal channel for having children within marriage is that they be generated by the husband, their father. In this particular and all-special case, the Child was God Himself, miraculously conceived in Mary, and through her, bestowed on Joseph her husband.

So it is that Jesus belonged to Joseph's family, and that is why the Saint should not be called the adoptive father of Jesus. It is true that his fatherhood has some resemblances to ordinary adoptive fatherhood, because Joseph received Jesus with fatherly love; but it is different in so many other respects that some other title should be used.

Should Joseph be called "putative father of Jesus"? This title, too, calls for explanation. We must keep in mind that it was part of Joseph's vocation to shield the reputation of both Mary and Jesus. Temporarily, he was to appear publicly as if he were the natural father of Jesus. "Putative" comes from the Latin *putare*, meaning "to think." The gospels never call Joseph the putative father of Jesus. They merely indicate, as the title indicates, that Joseph was publicly supposed for a time to be the natural father of our Lord. Of itself, this does not give St. Joseph any fatherly relationship to Jesus. It merely points out the public opinion. To give a parallel: If two persons walked together, man and boy, and if the on-lookers thought that the man was the boy's natural father, the man would be made in a sense the putative father, even though he might be a complete stranger to the boy who happened to be beside him.

All this means that Joseph somehow or other had a fatherly relationship to our Lord that was distinct from the wrong supposition of physical fatherhood as made by his neighbors. If Joseph's fatherhood were solely putative, then once the error had been explained away, the Saint would have no further relationship to Jesus, and this would be contrary to what the gospels tell us.

Strictly speaking, Joseph *was* the putative father of Jesus only during the period of our Lord's Hidden Life, until the time when Jesus claimed to be the natural son of God. No one is justified any longer in claiming that Joseph generated Jesus; hence, Joseph no longer *is* the putative father of our Lord.

This does not mean that we intend to derogate from the value of the title. We wish to point out that it does not explain in any positive sense what Joseph's relationship is. It does imply, however, a real honor in that the Saint was chosen by God to conceal the miracle of the Incarnation until it was revealed in the public preaching of our Lord.

Sometimes St. Joseph has been called "legal father" of Jesus. Is this title correct? Again, an answer cannot be made without proper distinctions. If the title means that the law considered Joseph to be the natural father of Jesus, then it means the same thing as "putative father." It might, of course, and usually does mean something more. It suggests that Joseph possessed all the legal rights of a human natural father of Jesus if such a one had existed. In this sense it is thoroughly correct.

The time-honored and highly popular "foster father" should fit into the requirements for an apt name for St. Joseph's fatherhood because it has been used so widely and therefore has been recognized as a proper title. None the less, it must be judged correct for what it says but incomplete for what it does not say. It indicates that Joseph accepted Jesus with the love of a fosterer, bound to his Son by links not of blood but of affection. Yet, "foster father" fails to tell us *why* this happened to St. Joseph. It does not express the fact that Joseph's position is vastly different from that of the ordinary human foster father who so often is also an adoptive father.

We always return to the one basic fact concerning the Holy Family. Jesus Christ was miraculously the son of Mary, the virgin wife of St. Joseph. Since God brought the marriage of Joseph and our Lady into existence to receive Jesus as its fruit, Joseph had a miraculous fatherhood, too, dependent on the fact of this marriage to our Lady.

Joseph's virginity helped to shape his fatherhood. By God's plan, as we have several times indicated, Jesus was to be born within a virginal marriage. Joseph's consent embraced first of all, his position as *husband* in the marriage and therefore father of any fruit it might have. Secondly, he consented to live with Mary as her *virginal* husband, and thereby made the marriage possible as it was divinely planned. His relinquishing of his marriage rights did not in any sense cause the Incarnation of Jesus, but it positively prepared for Christ's coming by bringing the union with our Lady into existence as both virginal and matrimonial.

Thus, it is from the virginal marriage that Joseph gets his fatherly rights over Jesus. Ultimately, too, it is from the same source that Joseph loves Jesus as his God-given Son, and that he is father of Jesus in every respect that he, a virginal man, can be such. These facts are the foundation of still another title, and probably the best for St. Joseph, "Virgin father of Jesus." St. Augustine was the first to use it in his writings some fifteen hundred years ago. Pope St. Pius X approved and indulgenced a prayer in which St. Joseph is called by this name.

One may logically ask whether we may say without qualification, "Joseph is the father of Jesus." There is no possibility in our own day for any fair-minded person to think that we claim Joseph as the natural father of Jesus; the facts of the gospel are too well known. If, then, in speech we have made it clear that we refer to the *spiritual* bonds between Joseph and Jesus, it would seem that no one can justly complain when at times Joseph is called "father of Jesus."

No less a person than Pope Leo XIII used this type of wording in his encyclical on St. Joseph, *Quamquam Pluries.* He first referred to Joseph, "who was father, as was supposed, of Jesus," and then added that the Saint is justly named patron of the Universal Church "because he was the husband of Mary *and the father of Jesus.*" We can also go back to Luke's texts and the precious sentence of Mary, "Son . . . Thy father and I have been searching for Thee" (Lk. 2:48).

Without seeking to quibble over words, something should be said concerning the senses in which Joseph is the father of Jesus. Certain statements ought to be avoided because of their vagueness and need for distinction. "Jesus had no earthly father" and "Joseph was not the real father of Jesus" are denaturing expressions that seem to deny all paternity to the Saint. Instead, he might rightly be pictured as "father in a true (or a real) sense" since his fatherhood exists analogously in the moral order. It would, however, be incorrect to claim that Joseph is father of our Lord in *the* real or *the* true or *the* full sense of the word. Fatherhood indicates first of all, the physical generation of the child and only secondarily, the support and upbringing. Since Joseph is not father of Jesus by generation, he is certainly not "father in the full sense."

When all the distinctions and difficulties have been brought forward and examined, the undoubtable fact remains that this is the most sublime and exalted fatherhood ever given a human being: the relationship of St. Joseph to the divine Son miraculously bestowed on him in and through his marriage. It will forever surpass all human fatherhoods in dignity because it concerns God in human form.

## Love That Rules Out Jealousy

The tableau of the three members of the Holy Family together in the cave at Bethlehem can bring to mind another important lesson for us. That is the lesson of a love so generous that it rules out all jealousy.

It is a prudent caution not to compare the relative merits of the saints, calculating which is greater. Such a warning normally applies in the instances of the heroic men and women whom we call "ordinary" saints. For Joseph and Mary, however, we reserve a special category, because their holiness so far surpasses that of others that no reasonable doubt can exist concerning their preeminence. Yet we can ask, why is it and how is it that jealousy would be excluded from the lives of two so holy? Joseph is first in authority in the Holy Family, yet he is also least in dignity—and we are certain that in his heart there never arose the slightest murmur, the least inward complaint why this was so, and why he as husband was not superior to Mary. Our reason for such a deduction is that such conduct would have been wholly out of keeping with Joseph's vocation. God would never have chosen a man for so intimate a relationship with holiness itself unless he acquitted himself worthily of the position.

The love of Joseph for Mary and for Jesus is always the answer. Our own love for God and for our neighbor is imperfect, full of dross that shows itself when our love is put to the test. Joseph's love and sacrifice of self was so intense in the cause of Mary and Jesus that it would permit no intrusion of self. Joseph realized with every fiber of his being that all he was, he was because of God's gift, and in this case God's gift came through Mary. Mary in her turn was thoroughly penetrated with the knowledge that God had "looked upon the lowliness of His handmaid." To her the "Almighty hath done wonders . . . being mindful of His mercy" (Lk. 1:48, 49, 55).

Joseph in his humility recognized this. The sad truth is that the rest of us do not follow his example, at least not in its fullness. To realize one's dependence on God would seem to be merely right reason, the acknowledgement of a fact staring us in the face. Adam and Eve both saw with utter clarity that all they were and all they had came from God, yet they rebelled and sinned. We, too, unfortunately, no matter how much evidence we have of God's munificent bounty in our regard, tend to forget the obligations of gratitude, and our rebellion shows up in the selfishness that misuses the gifts of God as if they were our own.

Our own jealousies and envies are part of this pride that forgets we are creatures of God. Envy shows itself as willful sadness because of the success of another, whether temporal or spiritual; it is looked on as diminishing our own good. For example, when another is praised, we feel disregarded and therefore envious of the other person. If envy is deliberate, it is sometimes accompanied by hatred, by detraction and calumny, and by joy at another's misfortune.

Jealousy appears as a love of our own good accompanied by a fear of being deprived of it, to such an extent that we depreciate others in an attempt to elevate ourselves.

Deliberate envy and jealousy in their serious manifestations can be controlled by the grace of God and our own desire to do so. However, we will find from experience that such unworthy feelings will recur despite our best efforts to combat them. These represent semideliberate thoughts, and we should recognize honestly that in part they are beyond our control. To that extent they represent concupiscence, and to that extent we are not responsible for them.

Our duty lies in combating all willfulness connected with them. While it is a good policy to scorn envy at its very first intimations, it is even better policy to distract the mind as much as possible. The reason is that these reactions begin as involuntary (in the supposition we are discussing). The less attention they receive, the more quickly they disappear. Deliberate brooding on them would, of course, be sinful and would strengthen them, but for that matter, deliberate and prolonged direct attack on them would strengthen them, too. The rule is always the same: The less attention they receive, the weaker they become.

Many persons are surprised to hear of a virtue that seems to be related to the vice of envy. This is called "emulation." It is a praiseworthy desire urging us to imitate, to equal, and possibly to surpass the good qualities of others. What differentiates it from the vice, however, is the added condition that our rivalry is conducted by means that are fair. Emulation has particular values in urging us to use others' good qualities as a stimulus to fight our own laziness. Provided our intention is right, we should have no worries about any such well ordered incentive.

For help in making our love grow in this self-sacrifice, we can always go in spirit to Jesus in the crib at Bethlehem, and contemplate Mary and Joseph kneeling together by His side—the three hearts united in the most perfect family love the world has ever known.

# 7.
# St. Joseph and the Exile

Once Jesus had been born, the full purpose of St. Joseph's vocation began to be realized. Joseph was in authority over his precious family as their affectionate protector and father, wisely looking out for their welfare and safety.

Eight days after our Lord's birth, the Child was circumcised. Luke mentions the fact, but does not say who officiated. We must remember that circumcision among the Jews was primarily a religious ceremony which had deep significance. The custom had existed in pagan tribes long before the time of Abraham, the father of all Jews, but Abraham under divine impulse had invested it with special religious meaning. As a symbolic mutilation, this sign of belonging to God was connected with the generative organ as a sacred part of the body. The Jews respected life and therefore respected the source of life, rightly looking on procreation as a function shared with God the Creator.

The fact that Jesus was circumcised is another indication of how fully He desired to be incorporated with human nature. Although in our Lord's day circumcision could be performed by one of the religious officials of the village or by the father of the family, we have good reason to suppose that Joseph did not delegate the rite to anyone else, but performed it himself. A child's name was customarily bestowed at the time of circumcision. The angel had told Joseph to name his God-given son Jesus. Most likely, then, this command of the angel implied that Joseph was to perform the circumcision as well as impose the name himself. We ourselves would add still another reason for Joseph's action: reverence for the body of Christ. Any one less worthy than Joseph should not have been given such a paternal duty, for Joseph alone possessed fatherly rights over Jesus.

Forty days after the birth of Christ, Jesus was presented in the temple at Jerusalem; the trip was about a five-mile journey north from Bethlehem. This presentation of the first-born was based on an old Jewish law that such a child belonged to God as a sacrifice, as a memorial of the miraculous delivery from Egypt. The parents could then buy back their son by paying a token price, usually five silver shekels, about three dollars and twenty-five cents. Luke does not specify the money, but limits himself to mentioning the mother's offering. According to the prescription the mother should offer a lamb and a turtledove unless she was poor, in which case the sacrifice was changed to "a pair of turtledoves or two young pigeons" (Lk. 2:24).

This was the occasion, too, when Mary was purified according to the Law. Much confusion still exists concerning the exact meaning of the Jewish laws of purification. They certainly were not equivalent to an imputation of sin, that is, a moral stain. Too many of the situations described in the Law are either inevitable in daily life or else are positively good in their moral aspect. Sin could hardly be claimed to exist in such instances.

For example, any contact with a dead body would bring on a temporary impurity, yet burying the dead was a duty and an act of mercy. In connection with some of the religious rites such as on the Day of Atonement, the very man who led the scapegoat into the wilderness incurred an impurity thereby. The reason in this case seems to have been that the scapegoat was symbolically laden with the sins of the people, and therefore uncleanness was produced by contact with it (Lev. 16).

This uncleanness, we must emphasize, was only legal or ceremonial. We have no parallel with the concept in modern religious customs. The moral and religious motive behind it was the awesome holiness of God. The Jewish law considered that certain external actions made one unworthy to approach God, in other words, unclean.

We do not know definitely why a mother after childbirth was considered unclean. For all the ancients, the origin of life was so mysterious that they could see no natural explanation for it. Often enough, they considered suprahuman powers as working on women, so that in superstitious awe mothers were segregated after childbirth. For the Jews, however, life was always seen as coming from God. A "sin-offering" or holocaust was offered Him in recognition of the fact. This certainly never meant that marital intercourse or childbirth was considered sinful. The only conclusion we are justified in drawing is that the mother after childbirth was *ceremonially* "unclean." It has been conjectured that perhaps the loss of blood connected with childbirth had something to do with this liturgical uncleanness, for the blood was considered as life-giving and life-containing.

A popular misapprehension still persists in the belief that the modern custom of churching women is similarly some form of purification after childbirth. Such an impression could hardly be more erroneous. The Church rite consists of a psalm, prayers of thanksgiving for safe childbirth, and the priest's blessing on the mother. Her action is a public prayer of gratitude for safe delivery, officially formulated by the Church in its liturgy.

The presentation of Jesus in the temple has traditionally been interpreted as the occasion when Jesus renewed the offering of Himself in His human nature to His Eternal Father. Mary and Joseph concurred in that offering, renewing for themselves, too, the consecration they had made of themselves to the fulfillment of God's will. We on our part can make our own spiritual oblation to imitate the action of the Holy Family. The perfection and utter completeness of their gift of self is something no doubt beyond our generosity, but to the limits of reasonable prudence, we should not be afraid to tell God to take ourselves, our loved ones, our interests, all that we are and all that we have, to be used solely in the cause of furthering God's glory and the good of souls.

## The Star of the Magi

In the preceding chapter we mentioned how different is the popular story of the first Christmas from the facts told or implied in the gospels. Much the same comment can be made concerning the visit of the Magi to the Holy Family at Bethlehem. The Magi were not kings, but rather astrologer priests of the Zoroastrian religion, as their name suggests. Their country of origin is obscure, although Arabia seems to have been the likely region. Matthew does not tell us how many they were, but we deduce that they were most probably three since three gifts are mentioned: gold, frankincense, and myrrh.

The question of the star of the Magi is even more involved. Popular opinion thinks of the star as a miraculous phenomenon which *led* the strangers to the place of Christ's birth. Even a cursory examination of Matthew's account shows that the gospel makes no such claim. "Jesus, then, having been born in Bethlehem of Judea in the days of King Herold, behold, wise men from the East arrived in Jerusalem, inquiring, 'Where is He who is born King of the Jews? for we have seen His star in the East, and have come to worship Him'" (Mt. 2:1–2). Herod inquired of the "chief priests and authorities of the nation" where the Messiah was to be born, and according to their information sent the Magi to Bethlehem (v. 8). "Having heard the king, they proceeded on their way, when, behold, the star which they had seen in the East went before them, until it came and rested above where the Child was" (Mt. 2:9). In other words, they came to Jerusalem on their own, having seen "His star" in their home country. They were sent to Bethlehem by King Herod, not by any direction of the star. Only when they were at their journey's end did the star make its reappearance and rest "above where the Child was."

We do not approve the interpretation that the account of the star of the Magi is merely symbolical, intended to teach a lesson but having no historical basis. It is too closely interwoven with the motivation and actions of the Magi. The "star" was a fact.

Whether or not the star was of miraculous origin is a controverted question. In favor of its being miraculous is the claim that the whole tenor of Matthew's story presents it as such, and the fact that it seems to have pointed out the dwelling-place of the infant Jesus. In this regard, incidentally, we might note that the phrase, "having entered the house," (Mt. 2:11) represents the translation of the Greek *oikeia* as "house," whereas it can just as well mean that the Magi entered "the dwelling-place." Testimony from the times of the primitive Church via St. Justin Martyr states that at the time the Magi arrived, Mary and Joseph still lived in the cave where Jesus had been born.

The difficulty with interpreting the star as miraculous is that so singular a phenomenon would have attracted widespread attention and would have counteracted what was evidently the divine plan of secrecy for Jesus. One of the solutions suggested is the supposition that the "star" was actually a normal astronomical sign *which to the Magi alone had meaning*. In their case God would have providentially used even their erroneous astrological beliefs as a means to bring them to the feet of the Christ-child.

This second theory looks on the Magi star as something natural, though definitely providential. We must grant that for many Catholic scripture scholars the star is interpreted as having been a special creation of God and therefore miraculous. None the less, this does not rule out the intrinsic probability of the opposite theory. In fact, it would appear that the natural-star theory has not been fully understood by Catholics. The main reason for this is that it was at one time backed by rationalist scholars as a means of discrediting the gospel account, and therefore has remained under suspicion because of the agnostics who at one time espoused this theory in one form or other.

The "natural-star theory" is connected closely enough with the story of St. Joseph's life to make it worth our while to see just what the theory says. Our guiding principle throughout is that a miracle is not to be accepted as such unless the gospel clearly says so—and in this case it does not—and until all reasonable efforts have been made to explain this particular event in the heavens as according to God's natural laws. Whether or not the germ idea originated in agnosticism, certainly it may now be held and pursued further according to thoroughly Christian principles.

This theory, then, claims that the "star" of the Magi was not actually a single star, technically speaking. The Bible is not a scientific textbook and is not to be expected to use exact astronomical terminology. The "star" represented a conjunction of three planets: Jupiter, Saturn, and Mars. This does *not* mean that the Magi would have seen a new or temporary star, or that the three planets would have looked like one great light. Instead, it would be something of significance *only to astrologers* (such as the Zoroastrian Magi were), who would attach meaning to planets in conjunction (that is, when passing each other and supposedly influencing mankind).

The facts are these:

(1) Jupiter and Saturn passed each other three times in 7 B.C. (in reverse directions)—an occurrence happening only once every hundred and twenty-five years;

(2) early in 6 B.C., Mars, Jupiter, and Saturn were grouped closely —an extremely rare occurrence, this time seen only once in every eight hundred and five years;

(3) these extraordinary conjunctions took place in the constellation Pisces, which the ancient astrologers called "House of the Hebrews." Celestial events taking place there were supposed to be of particular importance for the Jews;

(4) Saturn was also supposed to have special influence on Jewish destiny;

(5) granting that the Magi had heard of the expected Savior through knowledge of the Jewish scriptures and national expectations, they would then journey to the capital of Judaism, Jerusalem, to find more information. Their conduct when they asked Herod as to the whereabouts of the king of the Jews agrees with this hypothesis.

Zoroastrian principles held that such astrological portents indicated the birth of a great man. These tremendously unusual signs in Pisces, the part of the heavens set aside to reflect Jewish fortunes, would then be taken to indicate the birth of the Jewish Messiah. There is no difficulty in the supposition that God used even their erroneous pagan astrology as a means of rewarding their good will in seeking divine truth.

The star as it "rested above where the Child was" remains always a difficulty in any theory. It implies that the Magi made a night trip to Bethlehem from Jerusalem—a rather unusual venture for times when marauders were feared, or were the Magi in such great haste? Moreover, we always wonder why the inhabitants of Bethlehem did not see the star, too. If we restrict the star of the Magi to be nought else than a vision personally given to their intellects, all reason to discuss it as a "star" disappears.

On the other hand, the facts are that Mars had moved away from Jupiter and Saturn by April of 6 B.C. Venus could now be seen in the early morning southeastern sky in relatively the same grouping with Jupiter and Saturn that Mars had earlier formed. This could mean that as the Magi neared Bethlehem, they would have noticed the configuration of three planets (still in the "House of the Hebrews") similar to the conjunction they had seen at home. Their sign would then have been considered complete.

An approach to a scriptural problem which is so coldly logical as this may at first sight seem to destroy devotion. It actually intends nothing of the sort. God has not revealed all things to us except the main facts necessary for our salvation. We are perfectly at liberty (and are urged) to use our intelligence in seeking out answers to questions that remain unsolved. Divine truth will never suffer from any investigation of earthly truths, for truth is always one, and all truth comes from God. Our only caution must be that our attitude remains intellectually humble, not jumping to a hasty conclusion before all the evidence has been assembled and examined. In the case of an open question such as the present one, we have a timely example of the procedure to use in submitting provisory explanations for a gospel difficulty.

## God's Providence

Joseph welcomed the Magi, for he was head of the little household. His action is a lesson in hospitality for us, as he led the strangers to "the Child with Mary His mother" (Mt. 2:11). Another lesson appears immediately in the manner God mixes His normal with His extraordinary protection. According to the theory we are following, the Magi came to Bethlehem with little or no miraculous guidance. They were men of good will who obeyed their conscience as faithfully as they could. God chose them from among all men as the first Gentiles to see the Savior. On the other hand, when Herod plotted to kill the Child, God intervened directly, and no longer led them by His normal providence. The dream-vision of supernatural origin warned the Magi not to return to Herod, and a similar vision warned Joseph to take the Child and His mother and fly to Egypt.

For centuries Joseph's conduct in this respect has been held up as a model of faith. He could have made so many remonstrances. He could have alleged that God works miracles only as the exception. Therefore, why not outwit Herod some other way, which would not be too difficult once the knowledge of Herod's treachery was made known? If a miracle was to be worked, then why not a miraculous concealment of the Child without leaving Bethlehem, and this would be so easy for God? Why so distressing and even dangerous an alternative as exile into Egypt? Why Egypt?—and the supposed improvements on the divine plan could have been continued indefinitely.

God's ways in this respect certainly were not our ways. As far removed as we are from the exile into Egypt, we can admit that we ourselves still do not see the *necessity* for God to use such a plan. There was no necessity. God could have used this or a thousand other ruses to delude Herod and his henchmen.

We have repeatedly called attention to the fact that Joseph and Mary were called upon to exercise their faith as long as they lived on this earth. Here is certainly another instance. God in His providence treated them and handled their affairs no differently from our own cases. We never are able and will never be able to discern the master plan. God alone knows that and works out His providence accordingly.

Sometimes we complain with childish petulance at the dispositions of this providence. We are fully aware of the fact that God is watching over us for our best interests and can admit it to ourselves at times when no interests of ours, no pet schemes, are at stake. The moment when our plans are upset is the moment when we must be willing to sacrifice our whims. If we did not have the knowledge of faith that God is in His heavens, disposing all things sweetly, we might indeed have reason to grieve; but with that knowledge all just cause for complaint is removed. This does not mean that our recognition of God's providence will make such submission easy. The closer a plan or desire is to our heart, so much the more difficult will be our conformity to God's will, if God's plan crosses ours.

## Joseph's Emotional Maturity

St. Joseph's ready acceptance of God's will concerning the flight into Egypt is from the moral point of view an instance of high virtue. From the viewpoint of the development of human character, it would be called a manifestation of emotional maturity. Right religion is right reason. Again and again the dictates of conscience formed according to God's law prove themselves the best even when considered only naturally or from the viewpoint of temporal welfare. Emotional maturity, for that matter, amounts to another name for holiness if sought after with the right intention. No person can be completely a saint unless he or she is completely mature in emotional outlook. The same selfishness which blocks the attainment of sanctity is the selfishness that blocks true emotional maturity.

The knowledge of the requirements for such emotional balance is interesting and valuable in that it presents the requirements for submission to God's will, looked at from a different viewpoint. All the descriptions of emotional maturity reduce to one: the unruffled acceptance of reality. Whereas laziness and emphasis on self tend to make the individual domineer over his environment and attempt to rule over factors beyond his control, the acceptance of what happens to us means that we are willing to adjust our lives accordingly. This indicates in turn a liberty of mind and action that is a rare attainment indeed.

The interaction between the religious ideal and the secular ideal here appears even more forcibly if we list the qualities generally accepted as comprising the temperament of the person emotionally mature.

The list invariably begins with the requirement that we be able to love someone besides ourselves. Such unselfishness appears in the religious sphere as part of the virtue of charity, the love of the neighbor and the love of God carried to a point where self-interest is overruled. Another quality is the ability to face disappointments, which again means the ability to face reality. We must judge a situation as it is, not as we want it to be. The world around us determines our lives in the sense that we cannot change our environment. Whereas in the secular sphere this may lead to disappointment because one's own desires are thwarted, in the religious sphere it will be looked on instead as a sharing of the cross of Christ, a providential interference by God whereby the use of certain creatures is taken out of one's life.

A third quality of emotional maturity is the desire to cooperate with others, or in other words, the sense of personal responsibility in a common enterprise. This again is nothing else but a manifestation of the virtue of charity, the love of the neighbor that looks out for his welfare because he is made in the image and likeness of God.

The emotionally mature person makes effective use of his talents in decisive thinking—and this is in different form the doctrine on the right use of creation, the appreciation of the gifts God has given us. To waste talents is to waste the grace of God.

Again, the religious virtue of humility inclines us to realize our limitations, to place our dependence on God, to reckon ourselves at our true and proper value. This humility has its counterpart in the emotionally mature person who has temperate emotional reactions, restraining the flare-ups of wounded conceit; who profits by constructive criticism, being fully convinced that he is limited in his outlook and can afford therefore to learn from the suggestions of others; and who has enough of a sense of humor not to be upset by trifles, basing so constant and placid an attitude on the fact of God's ever-watchful providence over his efforts.

These qualities appeared in Joseph's conduct as he led his two precious charges on the lonesome road into Egypt. On the one hand, Joseph showed utter docility in accepting the angel's message to leave for exile. Joseph showed at the same time equal initiative within the limits of the divine command. He was not told precisely where to go, or exactly how long to stay. In all likelihood he settled down in the Jewish colony at Alexandria and used his carpentry as a means of supporting Mary and Jesus.

The exile lasted no more than three years, so we judge, because Archelaus, one of Herod's sons, was reigning in his father's stead when Joseph returned. The gospels shroud the rest of the Hidden Life of Jesus in silence with the terse yet pregnant phrase that Jesus was subject to Joseph and Mary. We do not possess even this comment concerning the nature of the exile—its duration, its location, Joseph's livelihood, the life of Mary with the Boy of two or three years.

Joseph's directions from the angel had been merely to stay in Egypt until another message came. We are again struck by the fact that God did not reveal to His dear ones what His wishes were for the future. The exile was to spread into a month or into many years, for all they knew. Obediently, he set himself to the task of making alien soil another homeland. When the message to go back to Palestine finally did arrive, he took up the return trail with the same utter docility mixed with equally bold initiative.

The gospels have given us so few insights into the workings of the mind of this man who was so important in God's plans that we are all the more grateful for Matthew's comment about Joseph's conduct on his return. "Hearing, however, that Archelaus was reigning in Judea in the place of his father Herod, he was afraid to return there" (Mt. 2:22). The danger that threatened the Christ-child's life must still have been very real. Prudently, not expecting further miracles, Joseph made his own plans not to remain in Judea, the southern portion of Palestine. This is again the mind at work of the just man "who was unwilling to expose her to publicity." After his own plans had been made to avoid returning to Bethlehem, the Saint received a final dream to corroborate his decision. Perhaps the dream suggested, too, that he go up the ninety miles back to Nazareth. At any rate Jesus, the son of Joseph, was forever to be called a Nazarene because he grew up in the town selected for Him by His father on earth.

# 8.
# St. Joseph's Trust

"The shades of evening had fallen on the earth before the two bands of men and women met at the accustomed halting place. Joseph was waiting for Mary, but Jesus was not with him. Mary's heart sank before she spoke. Joseph knew nothing. His unworthiness would have felt surprise if Jesus had accompanied him rather than His mother.

"They were suddenly alone, alone amidst the multitude, more lonely than two hearts had ever been since the sun set on Adam and Eve. Joseph was crushed to the very earth. The light went out in Mary's soul, and a more terrific spiritual desolation followed than any of the saints had ever known. What could it mean? Jesus was gone. . . .

"In the darkness alone, Mary and Joseph were treading the road again to the Holy City. Their feet were sore and weary. What matter? Their hearts were sorer and more weary. Had it all been a dream, a transitory thing?" (F. W. Faber, *The Foot of the Cross,* 152 ff.).

Father Faber does not exaggerate the meaning of the sorrow that God sent to Joseph and Mary when Jesus was lost in the temple through no fault of their own. For us it is all such a lesson, if only we accept Luke's gospel exactly as it reads. There is no escaping the fact, the hard fact, that God in His utter love for Mary and Joseph, none the less took Jesus from their presence; for all they knew, He was taken away for ever.

We complain so easily against God's will in our regard. Our faith shows up in all its weakness in times of trial. We slip into thoughts of self-pity, telling ourselves that we are somehow or other not the chosen ones of God, and evidently left out of His love because He has permitted trials to come into our life. The present incident of the loss of the Child Jesus bears meditating on our part again and again, simply to drive home deep into our consciousness the realization that God sent this trial to His two holiest of all souls; and His trials for us cannot mean an exclusion from His love. Involuntarily, despite all this we may still tend to think that the whole episode is some sort of make-believe, a gigantic hoax that could never have occurred. But it *did* occur as everlasting proof that God led Joseph and Mary in the blindness of faith and asked such a sacrifice of them for their own ultimate good—and for ours.

Joseph and Mary underwent a mutual trial at the time when Joseph was made aware of Mary's pregnancy. At that time God asked them to sacrifice their love for each other until He gave it back to them. On this occasion God asked them to sacrifice their love for God their Son, until again He would give Jesus back to them—but of this they could not be sure at the moment. Would Jesus ever come back?

The trip to Jerusalem mentioned in Luke's second chapter was evidently one of the annual pilgrimages which the Holy Family made to the temple. As far as they were concerned, it was to have been as uneventful as any trip before it. The fact that Jesus was in His twelfth year, or as some hold, had completed it, shows He was at the age when the faithful Jew began to be bound by the Law.

Traditionally, the loss of Jesus has been described as the loss of the "*Child* Jesus." Perhaps in this we are forgetting the customs of the time and place. Our Western notions have been permitted to seep into the interpretation of the episode. When we realize that Christ was but two or three years from what was considered a marriageable age, we will look on Him as if He were eighteen or twenty years old, as far as the maturity of our own day would be concerned. None the less, He was still under the jurisdiction of His parents, just as any eighteen-year-old would be today. The point we are making, however, is that His recognized maturity then was far, far greater than that of a boy of our own times, although He was still far from the age—thirty—deemed requisite for a religious teacher.

The custom seems to have existed that children were to return from the temple with one of their parents, attaching themselves to the men's or women's group until the caravan met for its rendezvous on the first evening. Joseph and Mary each thought that Jesus was with the other, and they did not discover the loss, as we know, until the day was over.

St. Luke's narrative vividly implies their worry and their haste in returning to Jerusalem to search for their Son. Our own sense of mystery is compounded by the fact that the loss stretched over three days. The precincts of the temple were not so large that the search could not have covered them within a few hours. We seem forced to conclude that Jesus deliberately hid Himself from His parents. When Jesus in His divine providence willed that they were to find Him, He was in the midst of the rabbis, "listening to them and asking them questions; and all His hearers were amazed at His understanding and His answers" (Lk. 2:46, 47).

At the time of the great feasts (such as this feast of the Passover), the rabbis would customarily give sermons on the Law in the temple areas. It was in the midst of one such group that Mary and Joseph found Jesus. What was unusual was that Jesus for all His youth was engaged in the discussion with the rabbis. His genius was already manifest.

But if the surprise of the onlookers was great, the surprise, even the shock, of Joseph and Mary was greater; "they were struck with astonishment." Mary, for all her knowledge of His divinity was still acutely conscious of her maternal position. From the precious few words conserved for us, none can convey more meaning of this consciousness of a true mother's heart. Nowhere else, too, can we find a more absolute indication of the love Mary bore for Joseph in his position as her husband and head of her family. "My Child, why hast Thou treated us so? Indeed, Thy father and I have been searching for Thee in great distress!" (Lk. 2:48).

Jesus' answer is reverent though still fraught with enigma. A divine command for God's reasons must ask for the sacrifice of the dearest ties of flesh and blood. Jesus' reply is a play on the word "father." Mary has asked Him why He has caused His father on earth such distress; Jesus asks a rhetorical question in return: "Did you not know that I must be about My Father's business?" or as the phrase can also mean, "Did you not know that I must be in My Father's house?" (Lk. 2:49).

The shock of Jesus' conduct in removing Himself from the obedience of His parents is perhaps one of the causes for their consternation. Again we see an instance of how God asks for faith in His word even though it apparently is contrary to other evidence. Mary and Joseph knew that our Lord's character had more than a mere human explanation. His conduct as they witnessed it in their daily lives bore out this knowledge even more. Now they were witnessing what at first sight looked like a species of insubordination, and their faith was called on to believe that it was not, and that God wanted it so. We must never forget that for both Joseph and Mary their knowledge of the divinity of their Son was an object of faith and not yet the intuitive vision of heaven.

## Conformity to God's Will

It is a commonplace to say that this episode is full of mystery. So often in scripture when we read of the trials to which people were subjected, we can partially understand the poignancy of their suffering at the time, but we are relieved of the burden of their doubt and mental darkness because we see how events finally transpired. We have the advantage of hindsight, knowing how God's providence showed itself.

In the case of Christ's loss in the temple, however, we ourselves are still left at a loss to have an adequate explanation—"adequate," that is, if we mean one whereby we understand *why* God brought this about, according to our own standards. Our own baffled ignorance at twenty centuries' distance can serve as a norm to give us some idea of what anguish and doubt Joseph and Mary felt. They had a love for Jesus both as their son and as their God which was unbelievably far above the love of the greatest saints. For all they could know, Christ's absence meant that His passion had already begun, that the enemies of God triumphed over Him, that the scripture prophecies of the man of sorrows were now being fulfilled. And Joseph and Mary could not be near to help Him, if that were so. This was another source of their worry and grief. Added to the love they bore Him, it made their sense of loss tremendous.

Particularly with regard to St. Joseph, our Lord's words in no way derogated from Joseph's parenthood. Jesus asked Joseph just as He asked Mary to believe and understand that this separation from them, together with its harrying doubt as to His whereabouts, had all been directly willed by God the Father. They were to believe that the cross was sent them by the same loving hand which had given them so loving a Son, that this action was for the good of mankind and for their own good, but ultimately that its goodness came from the fact that God willed it. In no wise did it reflect unfavorably upon the dignity of these parents, nor did it imply that they had been remiss in their duty. They were to realize, however, that the requirements of God's will might interfere with the orderly progression of family life as they had so happily known it.

Later in His public life, Jesus taught this lesson of conformity to God's will, even at the sacrifice of the nearest and dearest ties, on the occasion when "a certain woman from among the crowd raising her voice cried to Him, 'Blessed is the womb that bore Thee, and the breasts which thou didst suck!' 'Yes, indeed,' was His reply; 'blessed are they who listen to the Word of God, and observe it'" (Lk. 11:27, 28). Jesus' language here did not derogate from Mary's dignity or imply any lack of love on His part; He did teach, however, that God's will was to be the absolute norm of goodness and of blessedness, and implicitly, therefore, that His mother was blessed because of this. His love even for her was subordinated to the will of the Father.

What Jesus said of Mary in His Public Life had its parallel here in His boyhood on that day in the temple at Jerusalem. Now the reference was to St. Joseph, and Joseph was used as the occasion to teach the same lesson. The will of God the Father always must come first. The words of Jesus no more reflected unfavorably on St. Joseph's dignity than did His words to the woman in the crowd who praised Mary as His mother.

St. Augustine with his usual acuteness perceives this double aspect of Jesus' words and actions. "When Mary had said, 'Thy Father and I have been searching for Thee in great distress,' Jesus replied, 'Did you not know that I must be about My Father's business?' For He did not wish to be their son in such wise that He would not be understood to be the Son of God. The Son of God is from eternity the Son of God, having created these [His parents]. But the Son of man in time, born from the Virgin without the husband's seed had each of them for His parent. How do we prove this? Mary has already told us, 'Thy Father and I have been searching for Thee in great distress!'" (*Serm.* 51 [ML 38, 342] ).

"The fact of our Lord's words, 'I must be about My Father's business,' does not mean that God is His Father in such a way that He denies Joseph to be His father. How do we prove this? From scripture, which reads thus: '. . . and when He went down with them, He came to Nazareth, and rendered them submission'" (*ibid.* [ML 38, 343]).

To show how much importance he attaches to this incident, Augustine returns to it in at least a third place in his writings. "To show that He had a Father in addition to them, One who generated Him in addition to His mother, He replied to them, 'Why did you search for Me? Did you not know that I must be about My Father's business?' And again, lest by this statement He would be thought to have denied them as parents, the evangelist added, 'And He went down with them and came to Nazareth, and rendered them submission.' . . . To whom was He subject unless to His parents?" (*De nup. et concup.* 1, 11 [ML 44, 421] ).

## Confidence in God

This lesson of faith as Joseph and Mary exercised it at Jerusalem is again the lesson of absolute confidence in God's will. It has been the subject of innumerable writings, from the words of Jesus on trust in God through the libraries of commentary on the subject. For succinctness and warmth, the prayer of confidence composed by Blessed Claude de la Colombière seems to be unsurpassed. We reproduce it here with minor paraphrase, simply for its value in describing the ideal attitude of confidence in God.

"My God, I am so convinced that You keep watch over those who hope in You, and that we can want for nothing when we look for all from You, that I am resolved in the future to live free from every care, and to turn all my anxieties over to You. 'In peace, in the selfsame, I will sleep and I will rest; for Thou, O Lord, singularly hast settled me in hope' (Ps. 4:9).

"Men may deprive me of riches and of honor; sickness may take away my strength and the means of serving You; I may even lose Your grace by sin, but I shall never lose my confidence. I shall keep it till the last moment of my life, and at that moment all the powers of hell shall seek in vain to wrest it from me. 'In peace in the selfsame, I will sleep and I will rest.'

"Let others seek happiness in their wealth and in their talents; let them trust to the purity of their lives, the severity of their mortifications, the number of their good works, the fervor of their prayers. 'You, O Lord, singularly have settled me in hope.' As for me, O my Lord, all my confidence is my confidence itself. This confidence has never been in vain. No one has ever hoped in the Lord and has been confounded.

"I am sure, therefore, that I shall be eternally happy, since I firmly hope to be, and because it is from You, O God, that I hope for it. 'In

Thee, O Lord, have I hoped, let me never be confounded' (Ps. 30:1).

"I know, alas, I know only too well that I am frail and changeable. I know what temptation can do against the strongest virtue. I have seen the stars of heaven fall, and the pillars of the firmament totter; but this cannot frighten me. So long as I continue to hope, I shall be sheltered from all misfortune; and I am sure of hoping always, since I rely on You to sustain my confidence.

"Finally, I know that my confidence cannot be in vain, and that I shall never receive less than I have hoped for from You. Therefore, I hope that You will sustain me against my evil inclinations; I hope that You will protect me against the most furious assaults of the evil one; I hope that You will cause my weakness to triumph over my most powerful enemies. I know that You will love me always, and I hope I will love You forever in return. 'In Thee, O Lord, have I hoped. Let me never be confounded.' "

## The Joy of Joseph and Mary

We might obtain a very one-sided and incomplete impression of Joseph and Mary if we were to stop with the idea of the loss of Jesus and to go no further. Traditionally, the loss of Jesus in the temple has been listed among the seven major sorrows of both Mary and Joseph. We should not forget that the finding of the Child is listed among their seven outstanding joys.

All the tenor of the gospel accounts of the Holy Family suggests that Joseph, Mary, and Jesus were taken for granted by their neighbors as ordinary people. Jesus was strongly disliked by His enemies, but He was grudgingly given the respect owed to a man of exemplary character. The implication is that His parents were taken in the same light, too. "Is not this Jesus, the son of Joseph, whose father and mother we know?" (Jn. 6:42).

Persons who go through life with an unalterably gloomy and somber outlook are considered unusual or at least are shunned by their fellow men because of their moroseness. The clear evidence is that Jesus was considered serious, yet anything but morose. Otherwise, He would not have been able to win to Himself the love of so many hearts. We are certainly justified in extending this quality of attractiveness to include Joseph and Mary, for they were so close to Him. Their character could hardly have been repellent; they must have possessed an underlying basic cheerfulness in order to have made the impression they did.

Even if we felt that the gospel evidence does not imply this conclusion, we could arrive at it independently from a full understanding of the holiness of the three principals involved: Jesus, Mary, and Joseph. No three human natures ever lived in which such sanctity existed. Yet holiness must mean the perfection of virtue, and virtue in its turn is the full and harmonious development of human moral gifts and God-given grace. Sadness that is overindulged is certainly not a virtue. It can be a sham and an excuse for downright selfishness, and a further excuse for warped spiritual pride that turns into itself and away from God's joyous creation in order to find reassurance.

These principles clearly apply to the conduct of Joseph and Mary after the finding of Jesus. All along, they had understood well that the son whom God miraculously gave them was to be a man of sorrows. The prophecies made it clear enough for people of spiritual discernment that the Messiah would be a redeemer saving His people by means of suffering. In realizing this, however, Joseph and Mary both realized equally that such suffering was to be accomplished according to the will of the Eternal Father. Until such time as God made His will manifest, they would certainly have acted in a very imperfect way if they had given way to deliberate foreboding and unmitigated depression. The idea that Jesus had a grim future ahead of Him was counterbalanced by the fact that this future was chosen and controlled according to the providence of eternal Love itself. Then, too, the perfect faith of this perfect couple would show itself in their complete confidence that God in His goodness and power would eventually bring good out of evil.

For ourselves, we can glimpse some of the reasoning that gave Joseph and Mary this serene internal peace according to the acceptance of God's will. The serenity would be mirrored in cheerfulness in meeting the ups and downs of everyday life, with the small crosses or the great trials God might send.

### Cheerfulness

In our own lives we can make ample application of this lesson of cheerfulness based on the acceptance of God's will. The cheerful outlook carries with it so many advantages. Paramount among them is the encouragement and stimulation to persevere and to make progress. This does not mean, of course, that at every moment in every day we are consciously and explicitly forcing ourselves to be cheerful. Such conduct is impossible for human beings, given the normal inevitable swing of moods and reactions that must occur in meeting different occasions and different persons. We would be in grave error if we were to think that holiness demands extreme austerity of conduct.

No less a person than St. Thomas Aquinas strongly defends conduct that is properly cheerful and relaxed. In his discussion of the virtue of modesty (*Summa Theologica,* 2a 2ae, q. 168 ff.) he presents a well reasoned attitude toward the subject. Modesty, it should be noted, ultimately means moderation. Although it can refer to moderation in one's ambition or in one's dress, here we are using the term with respect to one's bodily actions and attitudes, and therefore with regard to cheerfulness.

Many persons in their religious and moral training have had ample emphasis placed on the serious responsibilities of observing God's law. Only too often, however, they are ignorant of the fact that virtue is not one-sided, and that relaxation and affability and friendly banter are called virtues just as legitimately as are humility and sober attention to the duties of one's state of life. It is because of this gap in the average corps of knowledge that St. Thomas' teaching about cheerfulness and wittiness is so valuable and deserves to be more widely known.

There are, of course, apparent objections toward the cheerful attitude, as if the optimistic and properly lighthearted outlook were at least imperfect if not sinful. Aquinas mentions a few. In the words of St. Ambrose, "Our Lord says, 'Woe to you who laugh now! for you shall mourn and weep!' (Lk. 6:25). Wherefore, I consider that all games, and not only excessive games should be avoided" (*De offic.* 1, 23 [ML 16:54]).

St. John Chrysostom has an even more severe denunciation. "It is not God but the devil who is the author of fun. Listen to what happened to those who played: 'The people sat down to eat and drink, and they rose up to play'" (Exod. 32:6; *Hom. 6 in Mt.* [MG 11:70]). In this mood they worshiped the golden calf which they had fashioned, and three thousand of them (according to the Hebrew text) were slain by the Levites as a punishment for their idolatry.

Against these somber words, which one would think must have some more benign interpretation, Aquinas counters with the words of Augustine, "I pray thee, spare thyself at times, for it becomes a wise person occasionally to relax the high pressure of his attention to work" (*De Musica* 2, 14 [ML 32:1116]). And this relaxation, St. Thomas adds, consists in playful words and deeds, in the cheerful *virtue* of wittiness.

There is an apt comparison between rest for the body and rest for the mind. Just as relaxation of the body gives it strength and enables it to return to its labors refreshed and vigorous again, so does pleasure and mental cheerfulness reinvigorate the soul. On this score the old legend tells us about St. John the Evangelist, who was playing with his disciples. Some of the bystanders were scandalized by such levity on the part of an apostle of the Lord. On seeing this, John asked a bowman to shoot an arrow. The man obeyed. John asked the bowman to repeat his action again and again, and how often could this be done? How tightly could the bow be bent? The answer was that the bow would break if it were bent too often and too far. John then drew the inference, obvious by now, that tension of the mind calls for relaxation.

Proper caution, of course, should be observed with regard to mental relaxation. It should not be sought in harmful or indecent deeds or words, nor should it take away the dignity belonging to the conduct of a human being. It should be proportioned to persons, times, and places, so that our conduct befits the hour.

As for St. Ambrose's comments, these must be understood in their original context: "Although jokes are at times fitting and pleasant, nevertheless they are not compatible with church order, since how can we have recourse to things not found in scripture?" Ambrose evidently referred to the exclusion of lightheartedness and irresponsibility in the discussion of sacred doctrine. Cicero's advice as a pagan orator is much along the same line. "When the audience is weary, it will be useful for the speaker to try something novel or amusing, provided that the joking be not incompatible with the gravity of the subject."

John Chrysostom's fulmination against fun as coming from the devil must be understood also in its context. He directed his criticism against those who made gaming and pleasure the whole pleasure of their lives. In this they were unbalanced and immoderate. We should indeed make use of play and fun, but in the same way as we make use of sleep and other kinds of rest, namely, at a time when we have already done our duty in serious matters.

Aquinas' comments on mirth and the lack of mirth bear repeating. Some holy persons, he says, are praised for their lack of mirth, and their austerity is called a virtue. None the less, whatever is against reason is a sin, and "it is against reason for a man to be burdensome to others by offering them no pleasure and by hindering their enjoyment. . . . Mirth is useful for the rest and the pleasure it affords. Austerity as a virtue does not exclude all virtuous pleasures, but only excessive ones."

Thus, we can conclude, reflection on the sorrow of Mary and Joseph when Jesus was lost in the temple helps us understand that God permits and even sends trials to all persons for His own good reasons and for their ultimate good. Reflection on the joy of Mary and Joseph when Jesus was restored to them reminds us that the close following of God's will does not rule out cheerfulness but instead at times actually demands it.

The example of Jesus would be, of course, the final proof for what we have been claiming. Perhaps, then, far more than mere curiosity has kept alive the question whether or not Jesus laughed. For centuries the point has been argued, and one wonders why more evidence has not been brought forward.

We can understand that the gospels had little space to recount humorous events about our Lord, for such was not their purpose. They had a serious message to transmit, and they were composed and edited accordingly. Someone has suggested, however, that the evidence of Jesus' cheerfulness and downright playfulness exists at least in the description of His blessing the children. Such little ones certainly did not shy away from Him. A gloomy martinet, overconscious of his adult dignity and of his profound message, could not be loved by such. Tiny tots look on playful fondling as a symbol of sincere love for them. Can we believe that Jesus acted with the children in any way other than the way that is still guaranteed to gain their love and their trust?

Another possible proof can be adduced in the words of Christ Himself. "The Son of Man has come eating and drinking; and they say, 'Look at Him! a man who is a glutton and a wineguzzler! a friend of publicans and sinners!'" (Mt. 11:19). Jesus was no stranger to banquets where He comported Himself in such a way as to attract sinners to Him and to scandalize the self-righteous. That fact speaks for itself with regard to His cheerfulness.

Still another proof would seem to be His conduct at the wedding feast at Cana. We are told by scholars knowing the times that such gatherings were quite noisy. Jesus worked the miracle of turning the water into wine—six stone water-jars, according to St. John (2:6), each holding two or three measures apiece. The "measure" was about ten gallons, so that some hundred and fifty gallons was the total amount. Jesus never countenanced intemperance, but His action on this occasion certainly did not condemn the merrymakers.

Closer to our own day, when examples of austere saints are placed before us, we must keep in mind several qualifications, as we mentioned earlier. It is possible that we do not possess the complete picture, especially when the saint in question is from a century when biographers felt it their duty to adjust their word portrait to the supposedly "proper" dimensions. God's grace adjusts itself to human temperament. There is no one set pattern, no rigid mold, from which the saint must emerge. The theological maxim holds here, "Grace builds on nature."

Fortunately for us, some of the exploits of St. Philip Neri have survived biographers' shears and have been saved for our own day. Here was a man gifted with mystic contemplation, yet also endowed with a sense of humor that enjoyed the practical joke. His humor was never unkind, never was raw—all accounts agree in that; but his humor was there, and he was a saint.

He was known to have invited a high-ranking churchman to dinner with his religious community, serving the guest a lone sardine; a religious who asked Philip (his superior) for permission to do penance publicly was told to wear a hair shirt inside out, *over* his normal clothing, and to ride horseback facing the rear, and this through the crowded streets of Rome; a baroness was enjoined to sing the *Miserere*, Psalm 50 (one of the penitential psalms) at a wedding reception! One can only conclude that holiness is not incompatible with humor. Would that we could somehow learn of the chuckles and smiles that must have been exchanged between Jesus, Mary, and Joseph!

# 9.
# *The Hidden Life*

It is paradoxical that we can say least about what is lengthiest in St. Joseph's life: the hidden years which he spent together with Mary and Jesus at Nazareth. Our only information is contained in the two cryptic verses of St. Luke. Jesus "went down with them and came to Nazareth, and rendered them submission. . . . and Jesus advanced in wisdom and age, and in grace with God and man" (Lk. 2:51, 52).

For centuries it has been a favorite task for preachers and writers to try to fathom the reasons for the Hidden Life. It is all well and good to point out that, humanly speaking, this was the preparation period before Jesus began His work; and that Jesus, who came on this earth to give us an example, wished to bless the obscurity of humdrum everyday family life; but these in themselves cannot be the final reasons. Ultimately we must say: God willed it. This is another manifestation of the will of the Father which Jesus obeyed throughout His life on earth, making it clear to us that obedience to God is itself a norm and motive for our conduct, and that no further consideration such as earthly "usefulness" is necessary.

The arithmetic of the Hidden Life is startling. According to the chronology we are following, Jesus was born in 6 B.C., and died in the spring of A.D. 30, some thirty-six years later. This would mean that the thirty-three years spent with Mary (and during most of these Joseph was alive) represented more than ninety percent of Jesus' life. He had come on this earth to found a Church to last for all time, and to give all men a perfect example. Yet because His Father willed it so, He remained in the background for so long a time.

The lesson of God-willed obscurity flows naturally from this fact. But can it not be mistakenly applied? There is always the possibility that we shrink from the reality of working in public or that we do not have the courage to stand before others and indicate our beliefs in word or deed. In such a case, if laziness or cowardice is the cause, it would be ill justified by an appeal to the hidden apostolate of Jesus. We must always keep in mind that His was *God*-willed obscurity. When the time came for His public manifestation, He did not shrink from the plain duty ahead of Him as He knew it to be.

On the other hand, contrary to what held true for Jesus, St. Joseph's obscurity seems to have been an essential part of Joseph's vocation. Too much emphasis on the father at Nazareth would have endangered the doctrine of our Lord's origin from the Father in heaven. Joseph was ever the servant of the mystery of the Incarnation, wholly expendable. His utter conformity to God's will shows us that if God had willed him to enter the active apostolate of preaching and teaching, no man would have equaled him in zeal in publicizing the cause of Christ.

The lesson of proper publicity for good causes needs to be inculcated particularly in our modern age. Perhaps in earlier times the members of the Church might well have remained on the sidelines, preferring not to know the world; but even if such a mode of action had justification in the past, it can certainly not be justified now as a general policy. In working for the salvation of the neighbor we must be prepared to "leave God for the sake of God," by giving up the peace of recollected contemplation as a necessary sacrifice when working in public for others. The public apostolate is as varied as individual states of life. It may extend to fewer or to more persons, but in all cases it means that we work for others. It does not include only the priest in his pulpit or confessional; the teaching brother in his classroom; the nun in hospital, social, or teaching work; or dedicated men and women in the mission fields; it includes, too, the housewife who instills the love of Christ into the hearts of little ones who are alternately full of charm or full of petulance; it includes the husband who gives an example in word and action to his fellows in industry or business or merchandising; it includes the businesswoman whose Catholic ideals are reflected in her everyday conduct. The list could be continued indefinitely. The main point for us to note is that a public apostolate is present in almost every person's life today. The only ones who seem to be excluded would be those incapacitated by age or sickness, but even these have their own apostolate of prayer; and to the degree permitted by their infirmity, they can give good example to the persons who come in contact with them.

The Holy Family's example of the Hidden Life at Nazareth should always vitalize the external apostolate. The more external activity to which we devote ourselves, so much the more must the interior spirit be cultivated. In that sense each of us should live and can always live a hidden life. While recognizing that we cannot pray always in explicit vocal prayer because of the physical limitations of the body and the distractions resulting from our duties, nevertheless we can preserve the interior spirit of prayer. In this sense we can "pray always." No matter what our occupation, none of us can afford to lose this interior spirit if we wish to keep closely united to God.

This spirit of prayer does not grow in us spontaneously. We cultivate it by sincere adherence to mental and vocal prayer, so that the habit of turning our heart to God is made practically a part of our character. When it becomes an ingrained habit, we are so much the better equipped to work for God, because the interior spirit is present, constantly invigorating our labors.

## St. Joseph as Protector

Meanwhile, to return to St. Joseph, we recall that during all those golden years when the "earthly trinity" lived under the same roof at Nazareth, Joseph was the head of this little family. Out of that position developed his patronage over the Universal Church and therefore his protection of everyone, everywhere.

In a later chapter we will present Leo XIII's encyclical on St. Joseph, reminding us that the Holy Family represented the infant Church. Jesus, the founder, was already there. Mary, the mother of the Church was present, too. Their little group was under the special protection of their father and husband, St. Joseph. Since, then, Joseph's guardianship at Nazareth was willed by God, his guardianship must be equally God-willed in being extended to the Church all over the world in all later centuries, for the Church is the extension of Jesus in His mystical body, and Mary is its mother and queen. Joseph's patronage in its fullest sense includes not only the actual members of the Church, but all those who were redeemed by Jesus —in every sense, all potential members of the Church, and therefore objects of Joseph's love and protection.

Second only to Mary, Joseph is the patron par excellence. His closeness to Mary and to Jesus means that he can offer them the merits of his heroic submission to God's will, united to the merits of our Lady and those won for us by Jesus in His human nature. Joseph's patronage of the Universal Church gives him a prominence no other angel or saint possesses, for no one else was husband of the Virgin Mary or father of Jesus on earth.

It is possible that we have heard the word "patron" used so often with regard to the saints that the precise meaning of the term fails to impress us. The idea goes back to the Roman "patron," one who exercised a sort of fatherly interest in helping a friend or a slave. Logically, patronage came to mean the prayerful protection exercised over us by our brothers and sisters in Christ, who have gone before us into heaven and to whom God has given a quasi-right of interceding for our welfare.

Hundreds of bishops, priests, and lay people signed petitions to the Holy See in the last century asking that the proclamation of Joseph's patronage be made. It is fortunate that from the very first the petitions used the words "Universal Church" instead of "Catholic Church." True as it is that "catholic" and "universal" mean the same, "catholic" has taken on a popular connotation more as a proper adjective designating the Church but not implying its universality. In other words the popular mind does not advert to the "universal" meaning of the word "catholic." At any rate, the choice of language was a happy one, and the Church documents have retained the wording of the original petitions, which emphasize St. Joseph as patron *of* all and *for* all.

Joseph's guardianship of the Holy Family, however, has not been restricted to a general protection of those entrusted to his charge. The Litany of St. Joseph, papal declaration, and even popular agreement have made him specifically a patron of the following classes (this list follows no order of preeminence):

*a*) model of workmen, because of himself he was a carpenter who supported his family by manual labor;

*b*) patron of the family, because he was entrusted with the safety of the most precious family that ever existed;

*c*) patron of the dying, because he died in the presence of Jesus and Mary, in the most ideal circumstances possible for a death in the friendship of God;

*d*) patron of the poor, because he experienced poverty as the head of the Holy Family, and this despite his efforts;

*e*) patron of the sick, again because of his closeness to Jesus and to Mary;

*f*) patron of virgins, because as the virginal husband of the virgin Mother of God he gave such an example of consecrating himself to God, and he protected the virginity of our Lady so admirably;

*g*) patron against demons, because of his powerful intercessory position with God, and his concern for the temporal and spiritual interests of the members of the Church placed under his protection;

*h*) patron of those who suffer financial reverses, because he came from the impoverished royal family of David;

*i*) patron of prayer and the interior life, because he knew the meaning of union with Mary and Jesus so intimately during the long years of close friendship with them;

*j*) patron of those in authority, because he, who was least in holiness at Nazareth, was placed over our Lord and our Lady, and he used his authority in the most detached manner possible, respecting its divine source and not abusing it for selfish personal aggrandizement as if it grew out of some intrinsic right in himself;

*k*) patron of interracial justice, because Joseph welcomed the Magi at Bethlehem, no matter what their country of origin might have been;

*l*) patron of exiles and displaced persons, because Joseph felt the pressures of exile in Egypt and the prejudice toward strangers, as well as the necessity of moving from Bethlehem to Egypt back to Bethlehem and then to Nazareth, in order to find a safe haven;

*m*) patron of fathers, because Joseph's fatherhood is the most sublime fatherhood ever given to any human being, and he is the worthiest of all fathers;

*n*) patron of husbands, because Joseph was married to the most perfect of all women, and since he had been chosen by God for this position, too, he is evidently the most perfect husband of the human race;

*o*) model for priests and religious, because his closeness to Mary and to Jesus makes him a pattern to imitate, especially in those dedicated to a closer following of Christ;

*p*) patron of travelers, because in his own life he led the Holy Family safely on so many journeys;

*q*) patron and model of devotion to Mary, because as her husband he was the closest human friend of our Lady, and possessed her love more intimately than any other human, and his closeness to Mary meant that he respected and understood her exalted sanctity in a way no one else could equal;

*r*) he has been officially proclaimed patron of Mexico (1555), Canada (1624), Bohemia (1655), the Chinese missions (1678), Belgium (1689), and patron of the Church's struggle against atheistic communism (1937).

## Joseph's Trade

It is commonly taken for granted that St. Joseph was a carpenter, and that this was the means of livelihood by which he supported Jesus and Mary. None the less, the fact of his carpentry cannot be accepted so definitely without further evidence. The gospel refers to Jesus as the son of the carpenter (Mt. 13:55). In the original Greek text this word is *tekton,* which as such merely means "craftsman." Theoretically, Joseph could have been any sort of craftsman, even one working in metal rather than wood.

However, the issue is decided in favor of carpentry because practically all primitive testimonies to the trade of Jesus speak of our Lord as a woodworker. Jesus logically adopted the trade of his father on earth, so that Joseph, too, must have been a carpenter. His work would have consisted in making wooden implements and furniture, for which he would be paid by barter rather than by money, according to the customs of his day.

## Zeal and the Hidden Life

The lessons taught by St. Joseph's hidden life have been variously enumerated as proper attitudes toward prayer, humility, obedience, obscurity, and work. Yet another can be added to the list, and that is the lesson of zeal. At first sight one might suppose that the remoteness of Nazareth from large-scale evangelization would hardly act as a spur toward the active apostolate. Deeper reflection, however, leads to a different conclusion. Since the three holiest people who ever walked the face of the earth made up the Holy Family, we are certain that their zeal must have been the most perfect of all. The fact that they were fulfilling God's will in a hidden corner of Galilee does not mean that their zeal was stifled. Instead, their very devotion in carrying out the plan of the Eternal Father was quickened and stimulated because of their zeal for God's cause and for the souls their actions would win. We must never forget that we are witnessing here the Savior Himself, in whose redemptive act Mary and Joseph are the most intimate cooperators in their proper grade and measure.

In our case, our zeal should be the overflow of our love of God and our neighbor in a heart that lives by faith; it should be our eager endeavor for God's cause.

True zeal is above all *constant,* so that we do not go up and down religiously according to our moods of changing fervor. We can, of course, have these moods and be influenced by them to *feel* at times very lazy in God's service; but these inconstancies come from our changing emotions and should not be ascribed necessarily to changes of will. The will to be steadfast is the important element.

True zeal is also *universal.* Like the members of the Holy Family we do not limit our interests to only those people or causes that please us, but we extend our prayers to cover the whole world and all its classes of people. Neither riches nor prestige nor youth nor attractiveness of personality are to be permitted to become norms that govern those for whom we work, because ultimately we are to work only for God.

True zeal is *prayerful.* We look to our own soul first, realizing that we cannot be a thoroughly successful channel for God's grace to flow to others unless we are striving to empty ourselves of self-love. To do this, we must have the spirit of prayer, praying for success in our work and realizing that God does the real work and that we are His instruments. According to this, our zeal will be *humble,* coming from a heart that knows its lowliness and its true station in God's sight.

Such a spirit gives God the credit for apostolic success; its zeal is absolutely *devoid of jealousy.* If we are doing all we can, we rejoice that others can do still more and in a better way, provided that our lesser results are not caused by our own negligence. One does not have to go far back into Church history to see the terrible damage done to God's cause and to His Church, even in the modern parish and school, because of jealousy.

In dealing with jealousy, however, we must be aware that our selfish feelings will remain. As fallible human beings, we tend to make our own everything we work for, no matter how noble it be, no matter that it ultimately is not ours to possess. Something of this fault shows up in working for God. Perhaps without deliberation we will suddenly realize that we have limited God's cause to our own horizons, and that we resent the apparent interference of someone hunting in what we have come to consider as our own preserves. These jealous reactions, it must again be emphasized, are not sinful as such, nor will they of themselves do harm to God's work provided only and always that we do not deliberately accept them or work according to them or encourage them to grow. Any labor we do in God's interest is always a sacred trust. Our own efforts are valuable only as long as we realize that they are part of the responsibility divinely confided to our care.

True zeal is also *obedient.* Otherwise it degenerates into work for self. If according to our state of life we are subject as priest to bishop or religious to superior or lay person working in a cooperative Catholic Action enterprise, in all such cases we subordinate our private likes and dislikes to the one great cause: God's interests.

No matter what our state of life we are to regulate the experience of our zeal according to the *prudent* advice of those in authority or those whose experience we can trust. Imprudent zeal does more harm than good. Imprudence shows itself in rash overconfidence in one's spiritual strength; in lack of patience in upbraiding others for their weakness; in deserting the charitable and time-tried methods of leading others by firm, gentle kindness gradually to their proper goals; in poor judgment concerning proper reserve in matters of modesty and chastity, according to person, time, and place; in thinking that we are now going to reform the whole world for all time as it has never been reformed before. Prudence, in short, must regulate our practice of zeal no less than all our other virtues. Ancient writers used to call prudence the *auriga virtutum*—"the charioteer of virtues," because it was to administer the rein or the whip at the proper time and in the proper measure.

Finally, our zeal must be manifested *according to our state of life*. Some of us will exercise it by means of prayer alone, if no external activity is possible, such as in the case of invalids and the aged. Some will exercise it in action limited to members of the family circle and close friends, since they are not in further contact with others; and some will exercise it in wide-ranging apostolic activity according as their health, talents, and duties permit.

Zeal thus becomes a duty to be fulfilled. There is always at least good example and prayer possible, a form of zeal available to everyone. Even in saying this, we should not disparage the value of good example and prayer with the denaturing adjective, or imply that it is the minimum by referring to it as "at least." A tremendous apostolate can lie hidden here. We think spontaneously of Ste. Thérèse of the Child Jesus, whose apostolate ranged so far beyond the limits of her Carmelite cloister that she has been declared patroness of the Catholic missions together with St. Francis Xavier.

The most noticeable manifestation of our zeal will, of course, be on the exterior, but the roots of it must be sunk deep in personal love for Jesus. This motivation is ably assisted by warm and sincere love of Mary and Joseph, because devotion to Joseph and Mary of its nature emphasizes the humanness and loveableness of Christ as our best friend.

In fine, our zeal must be a constant middle ground between the two extremes of burying ourselves in exterior work and caring too little about our own love of God (which is, incidentally, the only love of God over which we have direct control); and the opposite aim of care for ourselves, too selfishly thinking that we must work only for self and cannot take the risk of missing every little pet devotion and personal religious project.

The hidden life of Joseph which he led together with Jesus and Mary at Nazareth will always be the example of the perfect interior spirit of true zeal, toward which we can strive in order to reach full perfection.

# 10.
# St. Joseph's Death

Consistent with his unnoticed position of service of Jesus and Mary all during his life, St. Joseph was not given notice in the gospels in the record of his death. We can only reason to it, when and where it occurred.

The last time we explicitly hear of Joseph as a living member of the Holy Family is the occasion of the loss and finding of the Child Jesus in the temple at Jerusalem. Then, since Jesus "went down with them . . . and rendered them submission," the implication is that Jesus was an obedient son in the Holy Family for some time. This could also mean that Joseph was living for most of the Hidden Life; but we have no way of determining the span more exactly.

With the beginning of the Public Life of Jesus, we are quite certain that Joseph was already dead. At the marriage of Cana, which occurred in the early stages of Jesus' public apostolate, Mary and the disciples were mentioned by St. John as having been present, but Joseph's name was omitted. "After this [Jesus] went down to Capharnaum, Himself, His mother, His brethren, and His disciples; and they stayed there not many days" (Jn. 2:12). If Joseph had been living, he would have been present here, and would have been noted in a sentence that takes cognizance of Jesus' mother, His brethren, and His disciples.

This conclusion that Joseph died before the Public Life is confirmed by the full certainty that he was dead at the time of our Lord's crucifixion. It was then that Jesus gave Mary to John the evangelist. Evidently, Mary must have been a widow in her son's keeping. No other supposition would explain satisfactorily how or why she would have been entrusted to one who was not a blood relative.

With the rise of widespread devotion to St. Joseph, the Saint has for many centuries been considered as the patron of a happy death. The reason is easily evident. No man or woman ever had such a privilege as that of dying in the company of Jesus and Mary. No deathbed scene could ever have been attended by witnesses who were more consoling. It has been logical, then, to ask him to intercede for us that we, too, might imitate his death by breathing our last in the friendship of Jesus and Mary.

## Fears of Death

Such an attitude should engender deep confidence in the heart of anyone who has sincerely tried to serve God. None the less, many faithful followers of Christ have an engrossing fear of death that takes away their love of life and can be so grave as to lead to a complete desertion of religious duties because of actual terror, its resultant depression, and even semidespair. No one can accurately gauge the number of people who have such grievous fears. Available evidence suggests that they are many, far more than would be believed at first sight. Numerous cases exist where such a dread has been lifelong and yet was successfully concealed from close relatives and intimate friends.

All of us have our fears. We should use this fact as encouragement. There are only too many people who imagine that they are the only ones to react to fears which they are horrified to acknowledge publicly. They believe that they alone have the dread and sometimes even the panic that all is not well with them. Their fears then grow all the stronger in such a case, suggesting that their mental equipment is far below average normalcy, and that they are on the verge of mental collapse.

One such typical fear is this fear of death. On closer examination we find (as mentioned earlier) that it is often more the *fear* of a fear than the fear itself. As an example it is most apt because it is so common.

We should note, however, that in the case of death a certain amount of the right kind of fear is good for us. Both the Old and the New Testament carry passages of this sort. We are reminded in them to live well so as to die well. This is a positive fear, one that is constructive instead of discouraging. Reasonable and rational, it is based on the love of God, strengthening in us the love that is yet weak. If we did not have this wholesome respect for God's final call, summoning us at the time He has decreed, we would tend to grow careless in His service. In other words the utterable finality of death helps us to observe God's commandments.

There is, however, the other kind of fear of death, and this is actually not a religious fear. It is more correctly described as a fear based on emotional insecurity. This is the kind of fear that seems to make religious motives the source of terror; yet in fact religion should not be given such blame.

The emotional fear of death interprets death as a complete loss of *all* life. Frantically and fanatically, it holds tight to some apparent permanence in earthly living such as health, money, friends, family, and social prestige. Ultimately, because it is so emotional and so exaggerated, it is a lack of belief in God's justice no less than in His mercy. Throughout, it is negative, pessimistic, and discouraging.

This phrase, "lack of belief in God's justice," must be qualified, for "belief" as such is something intellectual. Our faith is based on reason. Yet this kind of fear of death is emotional and *therefore* is not essentially in our intellect. Should we not rather say that because it is so emotional, it masquerades *as if* it were a lack of faith?

It pretends to disbelieve God's mercy under the guise of protecting the rights of God's justice. Here again it masquerades as if it were defending God's justice. It emphasizes the punishments God has in store for us, completely sidestepping the fact that God, our loving and *just* Father, will be *at least* as rigorous in rewarding us for the good we have done as in punishing us for the evil we know He will see in us. In all such reactions, accordingly, this fear fails to give God even the reasonable minimum tribute of believing that He will keep His promises to deal with us fairly.

Throughout, it does not spur us on to greater generosity in loving God. Instead, it adds to a burden of anxiety and worry that can distract us from the one great commandment we have, to love God with our whole heart and our neighbor as ourself.

It seems a mistaken policy to counsel ourselves that such an irrational fear can be cured *and removed* at once, if at all. However, it is highly probable that with persevering prayer and the use of reasonable means it can be brought under control. A sort of check list can remind us of the principles we should follow, no matter what opposite emotional worry might rise to combat them. We suggest these ideas:

*a*) Do not blame the religious service of God as the source of a paralyzing fear of death.

*b*) Do not slacken religious service because of this fear of death.

*c*) Recall the promises of scripture mentioned again and again. Christ's words, "Let not your heart be troubled. You believe in God, believe also in Me. In My Father's house there are many abodes. If it were otherwise, I would have told you; for I am going in order to prepare a place for you" (Jn. 14:1–2.)

*d*) The Psalm: "Yet even now, my soul, leave thyself in God's hands; all my trust is in Him" (Ps. 61:6).

*e*) St. Peter: "Cast all your anxiety upon [God], because He cares for you" (1 Pet. 5:7).

*f*) St. Paul: "As it is written: 'Eye has not seen, nor ear heard, nor has it entered into the human heart, what God has prepared for those who love Him'" (1 Cor. 2:9).

*g*) Death is a mystery as far as our senses are concerned. For them it is perpetual sleep because they have no power to understand it. Therefore, it appears emotionally as a sort of annihilation but with our intellects we can go further than this. We can know that death has its purpose as God intended it, even though its full meaning is beyond us. Perhaps, then, it is better for us not to think about death, rather than to struggle in working out a positive satisfactory understanding of it. In other words, the possibility of comprehending the meaning of death while we are in this life is something like trying to understand the infinity of God or the mysteries of predestination.

*h*) Jesus died. Therefore, we, too, can accept death in imitation of Jesus and in union with Him. Death was not in God's first plan for the human race. In God's original plan death had been removed by a preternatural privilege, but sin changed that, and death became a penalty. Christ's death and resurrection have taken the sting out of this somber truth. In the words of the Preface of the mass for the dead, "In Christ, the hope of blessed resurrection shone forth, so that the promise of future immortality might console those whom the certainty of death saddens. For your faithful, Lord, life is changed, not taken away; and when the earthly home of this place of sojourn has been dissolved, eternal residence in heaven is ready and prepared."

*i*) Death comes to us all. Therefore, it is the natural, the normal, the universal human experience. The entire human race faces the problem of death with us; we are not alone.

*j*) If our fear of death is ultimately more a fear of God's judgment, we must remember that God asks of us a perfection of which we are capable. He does not demand the impossible task of equaling the awesome infinity of His goodness. If we go to God on His own reasonable terms, we should take Him at *His* word. This is part of the virtue of hope, to believe that God will keep His promises to reward us. Some of our fears about His judgment and the supposedly impossible perfection He will require of us imply that He is less generous and loving than even an average good man or woman would be!

*k*) A test exists to determine whether the fear of death is abnormal, scrupulous, and emotionally out of balance. If we fear dying with the death of a martyr for the truth, then such fear is definitely emotionally unbalanced. The martyr has the greatest reason for being sure of his or her crown. Fear of even the martyr's death betrays the fact that such insecurity exists that no amount of reasoning will ever convince it of God's mercy and lovableness.

*l*) God orders us to strive on this earth as if life went on forever. He alone is to determine the end. We are *commanded* by His moral law to use all ordinary good natural means needed to preserve life. God wants us to want to live.

*m*) When the "love of living" has disappeared, we should not be surprised if a strong emotional fear of death takes its place.

*n*) The discouraging fear of death is essentially egocentric. It forgets the lot of all the rest of mankind, that all will die. Thus, it betrays its selfishness as it narrowly worries only about itself, and again shows that it is essentially emotional and not an intellectual reaction.

*o*) We should not expect to "feel" full of faith and serenity concerning death. Our faith is being tried in this way, to make us live on the word of God. The answers of faith concerning death and God's care of us after death are certain. However, as far as these answers are concerned, our imagination and our emotional makeup not only give us no help; their blankness concerning a future in the next life which they cannot grasp positively holds us back. Even our intellect (understanding death in the natural order) gives us a very limited assurance of what is coming. Only faith in God's revealed word is complete in knowledge and complete in assurance; yet—to repeat—*faith is not something in the feelings. It is an assent of the mind; it is not felt in the emotions.*

*p*) Medical experts have stated what seems to be a rather common rule of thumb: "People fear death until they are actually dying, and then they accept the fact with a calmness which they never showed during life." The reason for this change in attitude is that the certain "now" replaces the uncertain future "when?" Once we know that death is close at hand and, as it were, "on schedule," it will be much easier for us to stop fearing it.

*q*) Ultimately, this paralyzing and frightening fear of death on the part of one whose life has been essentially good is a refusal to accept God's promise of reward. Looked at in this light, it reflects no great love of God or loyal belief in His word. Instead, it is a selfish stubbornness holding back from the trust of a child in the all-perfect and all-loving eternal Father of us all.

*r*) St. Joseph died in the presence of Jesus and Mary. The realization of the love of these three for each one of us is the basis of the indulgenced prayer that is so powerful in removing the unreasoning fear of death:

"Jesus, Mary, and Joseph, I give you my heart and my soul;
Jesus, Mary, and Joseph, assist me in my last agony;
Jesus, Mary, and Joseph, may I breathe forth my soul in peace with you."

When considered in these many ways according to right reason enlightened by the teachings of Jesus, death actually becomes our consolation. It puts all humans on the same level, proving that God in His infinite justice cannot be mocked by evildoers, and that the just will receive their rest and their reward.

Death is also our protection. If we thought that this life on earth would never end, we would selfishly let our love grow cold and would fail to live as we ought. The knowledge that earthly joys are temporary does not ruin them. It should make us accept them all the more securely because they are the passing reminders that eternal floods of goodness await us in God's plans.

This attitude is perfectly logical. We enjoy a thing all the more securely that we possess it or believe that we possess it. If we were to use the good things in this world with an eye only to their constant permanence with us, our pleasures would be vitiated by this very knowledge that they are passing, just as we in our own lives are passing. On the other hand, if we look on them according to proper perspective, realizing from the outset that they are only temporary, we gain all the more security. In using them we do not seek from them what they cannot give. We evaluate them at their proper grade and rank. That means we are in contact with a truth, a fact; and our sense of security increases proportionately.

Such are some of the thoughts that we can develop from the death of St. Joseph, particularly if we have been worried by the emotional and unreasoning fear of death. What of its aspect as a fear, and what of our related fears as well? When we look on it as a fear, we should remember that fear in itself is good. It is a normal response and preparation for imminent danger. It becomes abnormal only when we receive an excessive response to a stimulus, or when no stimulus exists, or when no stimulus can be discovered.

Our worries, then, whether they be about death or anything else, can be classified as part of our fears. They are a distortion of ability to plan for the future. Chronic worries in extreme form become anxiety. A fear of death shows that it is "anxious" if it is a vague, general apprehension even leading us to go out of our way to foster it. Then indeed we have the final proof that it is not from God as such. Our emotional nature has led us astray, and we will control and curb it best not by direct frontal attack but by oblique tactics of evasion.

We cannot remove an abnormal fear of death from our makeup by an act of the will, "I will *not!*" The indirect approach should be the method instead to follow. The less direct attention which we give to such fear, the weaker it will get in our consciousness, and so much the more freely will we devote our lives to the peaceful pursuit of living out the laws of God.

## The Spirit of Gratitude

When we go back in spirit to the deathbed of St. Joseph, it suggests to us another lesson—the spirit of thanksgiving. We reflect so easily, so spontaneously, that St. Joseph could look back on so much. True, he still had to live by blind faith, wondering just how the Redemption would be accomplished. He could know from the scriptural prophecies only that the son God had given him was the sign of contradiction and a man of sorrows and was the divine Savior. But on the other hand, he had all the conviction of his tremendous faith that God's plan was best, whatever it was. In the end, all the glory and triumph of Jesus would appear. For Joseph, that was sufficient. His peace would continue in the fact that God was telling him now that his work was finished on earth. To wish to linger would have been something selfish, a degree of self-will that would go contrary to what God knew was best. Joseph, like Mary and Jesus, was expendable in the fulfillment of the plan of the Redemption.

These thoughts in his heart would lead all the more to increase his spirit of thanksgiving. He had been given two gifts that were above all price: the love of Mary and of Jesus. He had been privileged to live with them daily. Trials and crosses there had been, and in his very death Joseph was being asked to add his faith in Jesus' future to the merits that would be joined with the merits of Jesus' redemption. The sum total of it all was still "Thank you, God."

Our own spirit of thanksgiving should imitate that of Joseph. It is easy to count up the gifts of God which we recognize as gifts. To fail to return gratitude for them is a fault which we cannot explain away. It is harder to count up the gifts of God which to us seem to be anything but gifts, because they are pain and suffering and sad disappointment and eventually death. None the less, they have all come to us from the hand of the one loving Father. The logic is inexorable when we look at it calmly: God is so good that He cannot send us anything that is not good for us. His goodness is so infinite that we cannot increase it in any way. It can manifest itself only by giving of itself to His creatures. Our own faith has to come into play and makes us convinced that the events God permits in our lives are all *gifts,* no matter how difficult we find it at the moment to discern their true nature. Eventually we will have all the evidence. There will be no doubts then that God's words were not fulfilled as He promised.

The Church has given us in the liturgy constant reminders and examples of a proper spirit of thanksgiving. Throughout the mass the phrases recur. Far less known, however, are the three prayers from the votive mass of thanksgiving, which can serve as a meditation in themselves, to lead us to a proper understanding of gratitude to God.

The Collect reads, "O God, of whose mercies there is no number and of whose goodness the treasure is without limit, we give thanks to Your benign majesty for the gifts bestowed, always asking Your kindness, so that while You grant their requests to those who beseech You, not deserting them, You would prepare them for future rewards."

In the Secret prayer, "Lord, receive the odor of this sacrifice together with thanksgiving; and grant that You would protect from all future adversity those whom You have deigned to hear and to keep safe; and may they advance in Your service and in Your love."

The Postcommunion is equally majestic. "O God, who never permits excessive affliction to befall anyone who hopes in You but gives a kindly hearing to our prayers, we give You thanks for the petitions and requests that have been granted, always devotedly begging of You that through these things we have received, we may merit to be delivered from all adversity."

"Gratitude" comes to us from the Latin word *gratus*, meaning "dear," "pleasing," "agreeable." Ultimately, this implies that when we are grateful, we realize that someone has done something for us that is pleasing or agreeable.

"Thanksgiving" has a different origin. It comes not from a Greek or Latin root, but from an old Anglo-Saxon word meaning "think." "Thanks," therefore showed that someone had many "thoughts" of a benefactor at heart.

We must be humble to be truly grateful. The cynical comment has been made that gratitude is a lively sense of favors received with an even more lively expectation of more favors to come. True thanksgiving is certainly far removed from such a caricature. The proud individual who is self-sufficient, conceited, vain, can never be sincerely thankful, because thanksgiving implies that one has received something that was not possessed beforehand, and therefore is dependent on the donor's beneficence.

Proud persons on the other hand pretend they can stand on their own two feet, that they do not need help from anyone else, and least of all from God. When they have received a benefit, they will not admit what is true: Someone did them a favor.

With God as with human beings there are three degrees of being grateful. The first is to admit to ourselves that a favor has been done. The second is to take notice of the favor, and that means to thank the one who did the kindness. The third degree means that we return the favor generously and graciously. The original gift cannot always be matched in value, but the goodness of heart with which it was given is always capable of being returned. When a favor is exchanged thus, the fine touch is to make it clear that this is not a matter of buying and selling, but of returning something that was first done out of generosity. Generosity can only be repaid by generosity.

These ideas hold true for our gratitude to God. If the spirit of thanksgiving is sincere in our hearts, we will express it often in our words and in our prayers. Most of all, we will show genuinely by our actions that we are genuinely grateful. Jesus has said that we can show our love for Him by keeping His commandments. The present instance is an application of the same rule. We manifest our gratitude to God by a more fervent spirit of generosity in striving to do good, and by a more sincere and trusting spirit of repentance and amendment when we have failed.

Our ideal will remain ever the same. After a lifetime imitating St. Joseph's spirit of thanksgiving, may we, too, arrive at the final solemn moment when we will complete our imitation with deepest thanksgiving to God as we wish to continue it forever in eternity.

# 11.
# St. Joseph and the Popes

St. Joseph's obscurity in the life of the Church has long since disappeared as far as formal recognition of his dignity and holiness is concerned. None the less, there still exists much ignorance of the statements of the Church concerning him. Undoubtedly the reason for this lies chiefly in the difficulty of locating the pertinent material and making it available for wide reading.

In the following pages we will present the major papal statements of the past century. (Nothing of importance exists before that time except individual decrees concerning liturgical honors for the Saint.) Because these papal directives and exhortations are frequently of such great importance, we are adding periodic commentaries to point out ideas of special interest. The format is so arranged that the documents themselves can be read independently of the commentary, according as a reader might wish.

* * *

The first of these great modern pronouncements was made on December 8, 1870, when Pope Pius IX placed the entire Catholic

Church under the patronage of St. Joseph with the title of Patron of the Universal Church. In two respects this decree was a milestone in Church history. Coming at a time when the Church's temporal fortunes were in a pitiful state, it marked the ebb of the reverses suffered by the papacy. At the same time it acted as a sort of signal for St. Joseph's meteoric rise to almost full recognition of his rightful status. Soon after he was proclaimed Patron of the Universal Church and honored as such, there began that era of papal prestige which has culminated in the present-day respect paid the Holy Father even by those whose religious affiliations lead them to oppose strongly any recognition of the Pope as a spiritual sovereign.

It is hard to dismiss as mere coincidence these two simultaneous processes—the rise of the Church together with the proclamation of Joseph's patronage of the Church. Yet the resurgence of the Church's prestige is a fact, and Joseph's patronage of it is a fact. Today we take both for granted. We ought not to be remiss in our gratitude to the memory of Pius IX for the decree which led to such important consequences for the Church and for the devotion to St. Joseph.

## *QUEMADMODUM DEUS*—PIUS IX

As Almighty God appointed Joseph, son of the patriarch Jacob, over all the land of Egypt to save grain for the people, so when the fulness of time was come and He was about to send on earth His only-begotten Son, the Savior of the world, He chose another Joseph, of whom the first Joseph had been the type, and whom He made the lord and chief of His household and possessions, the guardian of His choicest treasures.

Pius begins with the age-old comparison between Joseph of Egypt and Joseph of Nazareth. Yet we must remember that even though this parallel existed in Church literature since the Middle Ages, in line with Joseph's primitive obscurity the early Fathers of the Church never adverted to the symbolic likeness between the vocations of these two Josephs. The Fathers usually saw Joseph of Egypt as prefiguring the suffering Savior Jesus; they never explored the idea further to include the father of Jesus on earth. By including the comparison in this decree, Pius made it, as it were, official, and not just a private pious reflection without significant basis.

> So also [Joseph] had as his spouse the Immaculate Virgin Mary, and of her was born by the Holy Spirit, Jesus Christ our Lord, who in the sight of men deigned to be reputed the son of Joseph, and was subject to him.

The wording here carefully points out the miraculous virginal motherhood of our Lady, mystically espoused to the Holy Spirit even while espoused on earth by spiritual bonds to St. Joseph.

> And so it was that Him whom countless kings and prophets had of old desired to see, Joseph not only saw but conversed with, and embraced in paternal affection, and kissed, and most diligently reared—even Him whom the faithful were to receive as the bread that came down from heaven whereby they might obtain eternal life.

Two things are notable in this sentence: first, the paraphrase of our Lord's words in Luke 10:23, explicitly applied to St. Joseph: "Blessed are the eyes which see the things which you see! For I tell you that many prophets and kings desired to see the things that you see, and did not see them, and to hear the things that you hear, and did not hear them." Second and more notable, the detailed description of Joseph's affectionate fatherly duties toward Jesus. The Pope is certainly making it clear that Joseph manifested his love for Jesus!

> Because of this sublime dignity which God conferred on His most faithful servant the Church has always most highly honored and praised blessed Joseph next to his spouse, the Virgin Mother of God, and has besought his intercession in times of trouble.

Something of the formal and hyperbolistic style of legal documents enters into the decree at this point. In historical fact Joseph was not "always highly honored" in the Church for centuries. The word "always" mentioned here must be understood in context as "for a long time." But highly momentous is Pius IX's ranking of Joseph second only to Mary in intercessory power; implicitly, therefore, second to Mary in holiness. This can be said to be the first official recognition by the Church of Joseph's preeminence over other saints.

And now therefore, when in these most troublous times the Church is beset by enemies on every side and is weighed down by calamities so heavy that ungodly men assert that the gates of hell have at length prevailed against her, the venerable prelates of the Catholic world have presented to the Sovereign Pontiff their own petitions and those of the faithful committed to their charge, praying that he would deign to constitute St. Joseph Patron of the Universal Church. And this their prayer and desire was renewed by them even more earnestly at the Sacred Ecumenical Council of the Vatican.

The Pope here refers to at least three petitions. The first, signed by one hundred and eighteen bishops, asked that St. Joseph be declared Patron of the Universal Church—"he who was constituted by God as the guardian of His only-begotten Son and who tirelessly carried out toward Jesus and Mary the duties of father and husband with most loyal love and utmost diligence." Almost the same characterization was in a second petition signed by forty-three Superiors-general of various religious orders. A third petition bore two hundred and fifty-five signatures, thirty-eight cardinals' among them, including the future Leo XIII.

Accordingly, it has now pleased our most holy sovereign, Pius IX, Pope, deeply affected by the recent deplorable events, to comply with the desires of the prelates and to commit to St. Joseph's most powerful patronage himself and all the faithful. He therefore has declared St. Joseph Patron of the Universal Church. . . . (*Acta Sanctae Sedis*, 6, 193.)

Some writers have aptly commented that the Pope did not actually *constitute* St. Joseph Patron of the Church. Joseph's position as head of the Holy Family already gave him the duty of protecting the infant Church, as it were, at Nazareth. Pius IX's was more of an official proclamation and recognition of the fact. We should note, too, that this decree mentions the great power of St. Joseph's intercession.

* * *

The decree of 1870 was followed eight months later by a companion decree of July 7, 1871, which legislated for the liturgical observance of March 19, the feast of St. Joseph. Since so many of these regulations are now obsolete, having since been readjusted according to later liturgical reforms, we will not repeat them here. The doctrinal and historical part of the decree, however, is immensely valuable for its content.

## *INCLYTUM PATRIARCHAM*—PIUS IX

The Catholic Church rightly honors with its highest cultus and venerates with a feeling of deep reverence the illustrious patriarch blessed Joseph, now crowned with glory and honor in heaven, whom Almighty God, in preference to all His saints, willed on earth to be the chaste and true spouse of the Immaculate Virgin Mary as well as the putative father of His only-begotten Son. He indeed enriched him and filled him to overflowing with entirely unique graces, enabling him to execute most faithfully the duties of so sublime a state.

Nowhere else, even in the monumental encyclical of Leo XIII, can there be found in Church documents a paragraph which better summarizes the position of St. Joseph. These sentences must be ranked among the choicest ever uttered about the Saint. They teach that (1) Joseph is granted extremely high honors among the saints; (2) God predestined him for a unique vocation in preference to all other saints; (3) he was the genuine, virginal husband of Mary; (4) he fulfilled a fatherly position with respect to Jesus, being thought publicly to be Christ's natural father and acting with a father's rights; (5) his position is entirely unique; and (6) he carried out his duties with perfect fidelity to God's grace.

Wherefore, the Roman Pontiffs, Our predecessors, in order that they might daily increase and more ardently stimulate in the hearts of the Christian faithful a reverence and devotion for the holy patriarch, and that further they might exhort them to implore with the utmost confidence his intercession with God, have not failed to decree for him new and ever greater tokens of public veneration whenever the occasion served.

Among these let it suffice to call to mind Our predecessors of happy memory, Sixtus IV, who wished the feast of St. Joseph to be inserted in the Roman missal and breviary; Gregory XV, who by a decree of May 8, 1621, ordered that the feast should be observed in the whole world under a double precept;* Clement X, who on December 6, 1670, accorded to the feast the rite of a double of the second class; Clement XI, who by a decree of February 4, 1714, adorned the feast with a complete proper mass and office; and finally Benedict XIII, who by a decree published on December 19, 1726, ordered the name of the holy patriarch to be added to the Litany of the Saints.

We Ourselves, raised to the supreme Chair of Peter by the inscrutable design of God, and moved by the example of Our illustrious predecessors, as well as by the singular devotion which from youth itself We entertained toward the holy patriarch, have by a decree of September 10, 1847, extended with great joy of soul the feast of his Patronage to the whole Church, under the rite of double of the second class—a feast which was already being celebrated in many places by a special indult of the Holy See.

However, in these latter times in which a monstrous and most abominable war has been declared against the Church of Christ, the devotion of the faithful toward St. Joseph has grown and progressed to such an extent that from every direction innumerable and fervent petitions have once more reached Us. These were recently renewed during the Sacred Ecumenical Council of the Vatican by groups of the faithful, and—what is more important—by many of Our venerable brethren, the cardinals and bishops of the Holy Roman Church.

In their petitions they begged of Us that in these mournful days, as a safeguard against the evils which disturb Us on every side, We should more efficaciously implore the compassion of God through the merits and intercession of St. Joseph, declaring him Patron of the Universal Church. Accordingly, moved by these requests and after having invoked the divine light, We deemed it right that desires in such numbers and of such piety should be granted. . . . (*Acta Sanctae Sedis,* 6, 324.)

* * *

The next document concerning St. Joseph was the encyclical letter of Pope Leo XIII, *Quamquam Pluries,* issued on August 15, 1889. This is the greatest Church pronouncement ever made regarding the Saint. It secured for the devotion to St. Joseph a position in the

* That is, abstention from servile work, and obligatory attendance at mass, as a holyday of obligation. March 19 was not, however, made obligatory in the United States because the American bishops at a later date felt that the number of holydays should be kept to a minimum, since in a country so non-Catholic they were difficult to observe. An indult releasing March 19 from the holydays of the universal Church was granted by the Holy See to the III Plenary Council of Baltimore in 1884.

Church which completely obliterated any last vestiges of the centuries-old neglect of the Saint. In fact, the future liturgical and theological growth of the devotion can be only a development of the guiding principles of this encyclical.

In summary, Leo called attention to the deplorable anti-Catholic and anti-Christian atmosphere of his times, and stressed the need of appealing to Mary for help. Almost equally important, he stated, was the necessity of securing the intercession of St. Joseph, who in dignity and holiness is second only to our Lady. The Pope noted with approval the continued growth of devotion to the Saint and cited as its basis the position which Joseph held as the husband of Mary and the virginal father of Jesus.

## *QUAMQUAM PLURIES*—LEO XIII
(addressed to the bishops of the Church)

Although We have already ordered on several occasions that special prayers should be offered throughout the whole world and that Catholic interests should be recommended to God in a more earnest manner, let it not seem surprising to any one if at this time We judge that this duty should again be called to mind. In difficult times, particularly when it seems that the powers of darkness are able to make daring attempts to ruin Christianity, the Church has always been accustomed to call humbly upon God, her founder and champion, with greater earnestness and perseverance. In such times she has also sought aid from the saints who dwell in heaven, and principally from the august Virgin Mother of God, by whose patronage she knows that support in her trials will chiefly be afforded; for the fruit of such pious prayers and of hope in the divine bounty will sooner or later become manifest.

Now, venerable brethren, you have learned to understand the present age, hardly less calamitous to the Christian commonwealth than the very worst the world has hitherto experienced. Around us We behold faith, the foundation of all Christian virtues, perishing almost everywhere; We see charity waxing cold; youth growing up corrupted in morals and in doctrine; the Church of Jesus Christ attacked on every side with violence and rage; and a vicious war waged against the papacy. We behold, in fact, the very groundwork of religion overthrown by assaults that increase in violence from day to day. As for the depths of this catastrophe of our age and the ulterior schemes of the agitators, you yourselves know more than it behooves Us to put into words.

Amid such difficult and lamentable conditions the evils of our day have grown too great for human remedies. The only course left open is to seek a total cure through the divine power. Because of this, therefore, We deemed it advisable to call upon the piety of the faithful that they may implore the aid of Almighty God with greater earnestness and perseverance. But particularly, with the month of October now approaching—which elsewhere We have decreed should be dedicated to the Virgin Mary of the Rosary—We urgently exhort that during the present year the entire month be spent in the greatest possible devotion and piety. We know that a refuge for us is ever ready in the maternal bounty of the Virgin; and with no less certainty We know that our hopes in her are not in vain. If she has come a hundred times to aid the Christian commonwealth in times of need, why should we doubt that she will give new examples of her power and favor provided that humble and continued public prayers be offered? Assuredly, We believe that she will help us all the more wonderfully the longer the period is during which she desires us to implore her.

At this point the encyclical turns explicitly to St. Joseph.

But still another proposal remains to be made, venerable brethren, well aware as We are that you will diligently cooperate with Us here as you have always done in the past. In order, then, that God may show Himself more willing to grant our petitions and that He may aid His Church more promptly and bountifully in proportion as more numerous voices are raised to Him, We have deemed it highly expedient that the faithful should become accustomed to implore with special piety and trust, the aid of the Virgin Mother of God, associating with this devotion their supplication for the aid of Blessed Joseph, her most chaste spouse. Indubitable evidence exists for us to conclude that such a method of approach will be desirable and pleasing to the Virgin herself.

The encyclical strikingly urges that devotion to Mary should be linked with devotion to St. Joseph. The connection lies in the fact that devotion to Joseph is ultimately devotion to our Lady, because Joseph is all he is, because of and through Mary. For that matter, devotion to our Lady ultimately is devotion to our Lord, because Mary is all she is, because of and through Jesus. It is no original comment to add that "what God has joined together"—Jesus, Mary, and

Joseph—"man should not tear asunder." Devotion to all three goes hand in hand.

In this connection, concerning which We are about to make Our first public pronouncement, We are aware that the piety of the people is not only favorably inclined but is advancing, as it were, along a course already entered upon. For in times past, the endeavor of Roman Pontiffs has been gradually to extend the veneration of Joseph further and further, and to propagate it widely. In these latter days, however, We have seen that same veneration taking on everywhere unquestionably new stature, particularly after Our predecessor, Pius IX of happy memory, conformably with the requests of numerous bishops had declared this holy patriarch the Patron of the Universal Church. But precisely because it is highly advantageous that veneration for him be deeply rooted in Catholic morals and practices, We desire that the faithful be moved thereto no less by Our own voice and authority.

We could hardly ask a stronger recommendation from papal authority for the devotion to St. Joseph. "It is highly advantageous that veneration for him be deeply rooted in Catholic morals and practices." Now begins the most valuable section of the encyclical, as far as the theology of St. Joseph is concerned. Modern theology has merely developed, as we mentioned earlier, the principles set forth at this point.

There are special reasons why Blessed Joseph should be explicitly named the Patron of the Church and why the Church in turn should expect much from his patronage and guardianship. For he, indeed, was the husband of Mary and the father, as was supposed, of Jesus Christ.

The root of Joseph's patronage, then, lies in his double position as virginal husband of Mary and virginal father of Jesus.

From this arise all his dignity, grace, holiness, and glory.

The position of Joseph as husband and father gives him his unique *dignity* or worth. For this position he was given unique *grace,* and because he carried out his duties so perfectly, he increased in this grace. Because of his grace, he was equivalently *holy.* The fruits of his holiness will make themselves fully manifest in his *glory* here on earth and most of all in heaven. The encyclical continues with a formal enunciation of Joseph's preeminent dignity, and therefore of his holiness, for in his case the one follows from the other.

> The dignity of the Mother of God is certainly so sublime that nothing can surpass it; but none the less, since the bond of marriage existed between Joseph and the Blessed Virgin, *there can be no doubt that more than any other person he approached that supereminent dignity by which the Mother of God is raised far above all created natures.*

Leo always returns to Joseph's marriage with our Lady as the channel and the means whereby the Saint became what he was; but there is to be further and more detailed explanation why the marriage accomplished this. Before we proceed to this, one necessary qualification should be mentioned. When the encyclical says that the "Mother of God is raised far above all created natures," this statement must be understood in context with proper theological distinctions. Strictly speaking, Mary's nature is below the created human nature of Jesus, for in Jesus there is the union of the infinite, eternal, uncreated divine nature of the Second Person of the Blessed Trinity with the finite, temporal, and created nature of Jesus as man. These two natures are united in the divine Person, the Word of God. Therefore, the meaning of the encyclical is evidently that the "created natures," of which Mary's is the highest, represent *created beings,* human persons. To return to the encyclical:

> For marriage is the closest possible union and relationship whereby each spouse mutually participates in the goods of the other. Consequently, if God gave Joseph as a spouse to the Virgin. He assuredly gave him not only as a companion in life, a witness of her virginity, and the guardian of her honor, but also as a sharer in her exalted dignity by reason of the conjugal tie itself.

It is true that not every husband and wife mutually share dignity as Joseph and Mary did. In the case of this couple, however, their marriage had been brought into existence for the precise purpose of receiving and rearing the Son of God in human nature. That meant that the dignity of the marriage imparted dignity to the spouses. Joseph's vocation with regard to our Lady is set forth as a constant sharing with Mary. In accordance with the partnership of marriage,

Joseph shared common life with our Lady; he shared her virginity by testifying to the fact of her virginity and by himself living virginal; he shared her care for her reputation by guarding her honor as her legitimate husband; but most of all, he shared her exalted dignity as her husband, for God would not have chosen an unworthy man for a post so critically important with regard to the Incarnation and thereby, the Redemption. So much, then, for Joseph's relationship to Mary. Granted that his relationship to Jesus grows out of the marriage, Joseph's fatherhood is now described separately for the dignity it, too, possesses.

> Likewise, Joseph alone stands out in august dignity because he was the guardian of the Son of God by the divine appointment, and in the opinion of men was His father. As a consequence, the Word of God was modestly obedient to Joseph, was attentive to his commands, and paid to him every honor that children should render their parent.

Notably, the encyclical says, Joseph is *alone* in the absolutely unique relationship he holds toward Jesus. Divinely chosen for the task, he appeared publicly as the natural father of Jesus. But he was much more than that. He possessed some sort of actual fatherhood by spiritual bonds, because he was given jurisdiction over Jesus and he was treated by Jesus with "every honor that children should render their parent." Therefore, we must conclude, he was truly the father of Jesus, in every way a genuine father short of physical generation. Though he is not the natural father, the dignity of his spiritual paternal ties with the incarnate Son of God bestows on him the most sublime human fatherhood the human race can ever know.

The encyclical continues with the duties of St. Joseph as head of the Holy Family. That this position was for him something connatural, not arbitrary or artificial, flows from the fact that his duties were "prescribed by nature."

> From this double dignity, moreover [of husband and father], such duties arose as are prescribed by nature for the head of a household, so that Joseph was at once the legitimate and the natural guardian, preserver, and defender of the divine household over which he presided. These duties he fulfilled as long as he lived. Zealously he watched over his spouse and

her divine offspring with the most ardent love and constant solicitude. By his labor he regularly provided for both of them such necessities of life as food and clothing. In seeking a place of refuge he warded off that danger to their lives which had been engendered by the jealousy of a king. Amid the inconveniences of the journey and the bitterness of exile he continually showed himself the companion, the helper, the consoler of the Virgin and of Jesus.

Leo minces no words in setting forth the intimate bonds of affection that existed among the members of the Holy Family. Implicitly, we are reminded that holiness does not mean the smothering of love among humans, provided only that this love is centered in the love of God. The next step in the encyclical is to move from Joseph's position as head of the Holy Family into his patronage of the Universal Church, and the reasons why Joseph holds this position.

Moreover, the divine household, which Joseph governed just as with paternal authority, contained the beginnings of the new Church. The Virgin most holy is the mother of all Christians since she is the mother of Jesus and since she gave birth to them on the mount of Calvary amid the unspeakable sufferings of the Redeemer. Jesus is, as it were, the first-born of all Christians, who are His brothers by adoption and redemption. From these considerations we conclude that the blessed patriarch must regard all the multitude of Christians who constitute the Church as confided to his care in a certain special manner.

This is his numberless family, scattered throughout all lands, over which he rules with a sort of paternal authority, because he is the husband of Mary and the father of Jesus Christ. Thus, it is conformable to reason and in every way becoming to Blessed Joseph that as once it was his sacred trust to guard with watchful care the family of Nazareth, no matter what befell, so now, by virtue of his heavenly patronage he is in turn to protect and to defend the Church of Christ.

The wording in this paragraph is interesting to note. Joseph is said to govern the Holy Family "*as with* paternal authority." This restriction indicates that Joseph's authority as father is analogous to the authority of a natural father who has generated his son by physical generation, which Joseph did not do. A second reason for the analogous language is that Joseph did not and could not rule over Jesus with jurisdiction in the strictest sense, even while by the natural law Jesus was subject in His human nature to parental obedience. It is impossible that any creature of himself could ever gain true authority over his Creator. In the case of Joseph as well as of Mary, Jesus freely submitted Himself to them as their son, rendering true obedience to them of His own will.

Also striking is the fact that Pope Leo refers to St. Joseph simply as "the father of Jesus Christ," with none of the usual qualifiers added. Evidently, there should be no fear that the term "father of Jesus" will be misunderstood provided that one has early made clear the correct meaning of the term as it applies to St. Joseph. The encyclical continues:

> The statements made here, venerable brethren, as you will readily perceive, are confirmed by what We shall further set forth. Conformably, namely, with the Church's sacred liturgy the opinion has been held by not a few Fathers of the Church that the ancient Joseph, son of the patriarch Jacob, foreshadowed both in person and in office our own St. Joseph.

The reference to the "Fathers of the Church" applies to later writers who are called "Fathers" in a wider sense of the word, namely, men who were living already in the Middle Ages. Earlier Fathers did not advert to the comparison between Joseph of Egypt and Joseph of Nazareth.

> By his glory he was a prototype of the grandeur of the future guardian of the Holy Family. In addition to the circumstances that both men bore the same name—a name by no means devoid of significance—it is well known to you that they resembled each other very closely in other ways as well. Notable in this regard are the facts that the earlier Joseph received special favor and benevolence from his lord, and that when placed by him as ruler over his household, fortune and prosperity abundantly accrued to the master's house because of Joseph.
>
> There was even a more evident similarity when by the king's order he was given supreme power over the entire kingdom. When calamity brought on a deficient harvest and a scarcity of grain, he exercised such excellent foresight in behalf of the Egyptians and their neighbors that the king decreed he should be styled "savior of the world." Thus, in that

ancient patriarch we may recognize the distinct image of St. Joseph. As the one was prosperous and successful in the domestic concerns of his lord and in an exceptional manner was set over the whole kingdom, so the other, destined to guard the name of Christ, could well be chosen to defend and to protect the Church, which is truly the house of God and the kingdom of God on earth.

The encyclical now sketches the patronage of St. Joseph as it extends to individual classes of people in the Church. We note, however, that this in turn is nothing else than the application of Joseph's patronage of the Universal Church. If he is the patron of the Universal Church, he is therefore the universal patron of the Church—of everyone, everywhere in it, for the Church itself is for all.

This is the reason [namely, Joseph's position as head of the Holy Family] why all the faithful of all places and ranks commend and confide themselves to the guardianship of Blessed Joseph. In Joseph fathers of families have an eminent model of paternal care and providence. Married couples find in him the perfect image of love, harmony, and conjugal loyalty. Virgins can look to him for their pattern and as the guardian of virginal integrity. With the picture of Joseph set before them, those of noble lineage can learn to preserve their dignity even under adverse circumstances. Let the wealthy understand what goods they should chiefly seek and earnestly amass, while with no less special right the needy, the laborers, and all possessed of modest means should fly to his protection and learn to imitate him. Joseph was of royal blood; he was espoused to the greatest and the holiest of all womankind; he was the father, as was supposed, of the Son of God. Nevertheless, he devoted his life to labor, and by his hands and skill produced whatever was necessary for those dependent on him.

The encyclical from this point to its conclusion is concerned with an exhortation to workmen as well as further urgings to all the faithful to celebrate the feast of St. Joseph as devoutly as possible.

Therefore, if truth be sought, the condition of those reduced to slender means is not disgraceful. The labor of craftsmen, far from being dishonorable, can by virtue be even greatly ennobled. Joseph, content with what was his own, little as it doubtless was, bore with calm and dignified spirit the straitened circumstances necessarily connected with his meager means of livelihood. This was conformable to the example of his son, who having accepted the form of a servant, while being Lord of all, willingly subjected Himself to the utmost indigence and poverty.

Considerations such as these will serve to encourage and tranquillize the poor and all those who live by the labor of their hands. Nevertheless, although it is permitted them to rise from a condition of want to one of well-being, provided violation of justice is excluded, yet both justice and reason forbid the destruction of that order which divine providence has ordained. On the contrary, it is foolish to have recourse to violence, and to seek to better existing conditions by sedition and revolt. In most cases these produce only greater evils than those which they were meant to cure. If the poor wish to act wisely, let them not believe the promises of seditious men, but let them trust in the example and patronage of St. Joseph, and in the maternal care of the Church, which daily becomes more solicitious for their welfare.

Accordingly, venerable brethren, relying mainly on your episcopal authority and zeal, and confident that the truly good and pious will of their own desire and volition perform more numerous and signal acts than such merely as are demanded of them, We decree that during the month of October a prayer to St. Joseph shall be added to the recitation of the Rosary.

It was from this mandate in the encyclical that our present custom originated of daily reciting the prayer to St. Joseph, "We have recourse to thee," after the Rosary during October.

Concerning the Rosary, we have elsewhere already legislated, but a copy of the prayer to St. Joseph is sent to you along with this letter. We decree that this order shall be observed in future years in perpetuity. To those who shall piously recite this prayer, We grant them singly an indulgence of seven years and seven times forty days for each recitation.

Salutary and deserving of highest commendation is the practice of consecrating the month of March by daily exercises of piety in honor of the holy patriarch. That indeed has already been observed in many places. But wherever it cannot readily be accomplished, We desire that preceding the feast of St. Joseph, a triduum of prayers should be held in the principal church of each city. In localities where the nineteenth day of March, sacred to Blessed Joseph, is not included among the feasts of obligation, We exhort all voluntarily to keep holy this day by private exercises of devotion in honor of our heavenly patron, and to do this with the same zeal as if they were obeying a precept.

Meanwhile, as a promise of heavenly favors and as a testimony of Our benevolence toward you, venerable brethren, and toward your clergy and your people, We most lovingly bestow on you the apostolic blessing in the Lord.

Given at Rome at St. Peter's, the fifteenth day of August, 1889, the twelfth year of Our pontificate. (*Acta Sanctae Sedis* 22, 65.)

* * *

In 1892 Leo XIII officially encouraged the devotion to the Holy Family. In the following excerpt, which represents the pertinent portion of the Pope's apostolic brief on this subject (*Neminem Fugit*), Leo clearly states that St. Joseph participated intimately in the supreme dignity of the Holy Family. Practically this entire passage has been adopted by the Church as part of the divine office for the feast of the Holy Family. It begins with a reference to the critical importance of healthy family life.

## *NEMINEM FUGIT*—LEO XIII

It is a fact apparent to all that the welfare of the individual and of the state is in a special manner dependent on the family. Insofar as virtue has struck deep roots within the home and the character of children has been influenced in accordance with religious precepts by the teaching and example of parents, the common interest will be benefited. Consequently, it is of utmost importance, not only that the society of the home be established holily, but also that it be ruled by holy laws, and that the spirit of religion and the standard of Christian living be diligently and steadfastly fostered there.

Hence, when God in His mercy decided to carry out the work of man's redemption, so long expected through the centuries, He arranged to perform His task in such a way that in its beginnings it might show forth to the world the august spectacle of a divinely founded family. In this all men were to behold the perfect exemplar of domestic society, as well as of all virtue and holiness.

Leo teaches that the Holy Family is the unique and superlative example of virtue and perfection, shared by Jesus with Mary and Joseph. Joseph thus belongs to the privileged circle of the three examples of the greatest holiness the world has ever witnessed. Moreover, this family was brought into existence by God for its very special purpose: "He arranged to perform His task in such a way."

> Such indeed was the family of Nazareth. In its bosom was concealed the Sun of justice, awaiting in anticipation the time when His full splendors should shine on all the nations—Christ our God, our Savior, together with His virgin mother and Joseph, that most blessed man who exercised the rights of father over Jesus.
>
> We cannot doubt, then, that all the glories of domestic life, taking their origin in mutual charity, saintly character, and the exercise of piety, were without exception manifested in a superlative degree by the Holy Family as a pattern for all other families to imitate.

We italicize the next key words, in order to show the emphasis Leo places on the purpose of the Holy Family as the family for all families to imitate.

> *To this very end* a benign providence had established the Holy Family, in order that *all* Christians in *whatever* walk of life or situation might have a reason and an *incentive* to practice *every* virtue, provided that they fix their gaze on the Holy Family. In Joseph, therefore, heads of the household are blessed with the unsurpassed model of fatherly watchfulness and care. In the holy Virgin Mother of God, mothers possess an extraordinary ideal of love, modesty, submission, and perfect loyalty. In Jesus, who "rendered them submission," children have before them the divine picture of obedience to admire, venerate, and copy.

This paragraph has special application for those who might think that the Holy Family is not capable of being a true model for the modern Christian family. Joseph and Mary, such persons say, did not use their marriage rights since theirs was a virginal marriage; hence, they can hardly serve as examples for husbands and wives who symbolize their love in marital physical union in accordance with God's laws.

As already suggested in an earlier chapter, the answer to the difficulty should be almost evident. None of us as individuals ever finds an exact duplicate of our personality reflected in circumstances exactly the same as those amid which we are living. In every case we must *apply* the lesson. Some of its elements fit, some do not. So, too, here. The lesson of Joseph and Mary is shown in their spirit of mutual, selfless love. This is the spirit which must be present in the home if family life is to prosper. Without such love, there can be no meaningful symbolism of mutual living and mutual giving. Joesph and Mary lead the way in their spirit of oneness.

Let those who are nobly born learn from this family of royal blood how to moderate their conduct in prosperity as well as to retain their self-respect in adversity. Let the wealthy understand how greatly virtue is to be preferred to riches. Workers, and all who are deeply embittered owing to reduced circumstances and a lowered standard of living, particularly in these times, will not lack reason for rejoicing over the lot that has befallen them rather than bewailing it, provided they will but turn their gaze on the blessed members of that Holy Family. In common with them they are subject to labor, and with them they have their common cares of everyday life.

Joseph, too, was bound to find ways and means of wresting a livelihood out of his earnings, while the very hands of God plied the tools of a carpenter. Nor, indeed, is there reason for us to wonder at those prudent men of affluence who in the past have wished to put away their wealth and to choose instead poverty with Jesus, Mary, and Joseph.

In view of these considerations we may say that veneration of the Holy Family, if early introduced into the Catholic home, will steadily gain in vigor. . . . Nothing, in fact, can be conceived more helpful or effective for Christian families than the example of the Holy Family, embracing as it does the perfection and fulfillment of all domestic virtues.

When thus invoked, may Jesus, Mary, and Joseph take their place in the family circle as its propitious patrons. May they foster charity, mould character, and encourage the practice of virtue through imitation of their example; and by sweetening the burdens of this life which everywhere encompass us, may they render them more easy to bear.

Given at Rome, at St. Peter's, under the seal of the Fisherman, June 14, 1892, the fifteenth year of Our pontificate.

* * *

In 1920 Pope Benedict XV issued a special *Motu Proprio* singling out St. Joseph as the patron of workmen. In it he called attention to the fact that fifty years had elapsed since St. Joseph had been declared Patron of the Universal Church. While deploring the great damage to moral conduct which resulted from the First World War, the Pope urged devotion to St. Joseph as a remedy for the problems which were beginning to assume startling proportions at the time. He particularly recommended to the faithful the devotion to the Holy Family and the devotion to St. Joseph as patron of the dying.

## *BONUM SANE*—BENEDICT XV

It was good and salutary indeed for the Christian commonwealth that Our predecessor, Pius IX of immortal memory, solemnly declared the most chaste spouse of the Virgin Mary and the foster father of the Incarnate Word, St. Joseph, to be the Patron of the Universal Church. But now that the fiftieth anniversary of this happy event will occur next December, We consider it useful and opportune that it should be worthily celebrated by the whole Catholic world.

Casting Our glance over the past fifty years, We behold the wonderfully flourishing conditions of pious institutions which bear witness to the manner in which devotion to the holy patriarch has been gradually developing among the faithful. When further, then, We consider the calamities afflicting the human race today, We cannot fail to realize how opportune it is to increase this devotion and to spread it ever more widely throughout Christian peoples.

In our encyclical, "On the Reconciliation of Christian Peace," following the cruel war, We indicated what was necessary to establish order and tranquillity everywhere. In particular, consideration was given by Us to the civil relations that exist between nations and between individuals. Yet today the treatment of another cause cf disturbance, much more serious, becomes imperative. There is question now of an evil that has crept into the very heart of society. For the scourge of war had been laid on the human race at the very moment it had become profoundly infected with naturalism—that great worldly plague which, wherever it enters, lessens the desire of heavenly things, extinguishes the flame of divine love, and deprives man of the healing and elevating grace of Christ, leaving him without the light of faith, dependent on the weak and corrupt resources of nature and the slave of unbridled human passion.

Thus it happened that many devoted themselves solely to the acquisition of worldly goods. Moreover, while the contest between the wealthy and the proletariat had already become acute, class hatred now became still more grave by reason of the length and severity of the war, for while this on the one hand brought intolerable privation to the masses, on the other it rapidly made fortunes for the few.

Then, too, the holiness of conjugal fidelity and respect for paternal authority were often grievously transgressed during the war. The remoteness of one spouse served to relax the bond of duty to the other, and the absence of a watchful eye gave rise to freer and more indulgent conduct. More particularly was this notable among younger women. Sincerely to be regretted, therefore, is the fact that public morals have become far more corrupt and depraved than they had previously been, and for this very reason, too, the so-called "social question" has reached an intensity which causes one to fear the gravest of evils.

In the wishful thinking and expectations of the seditious members of society there has consequently been maturing the advent of a certain universal commonwealth that is to be founded on absolute equality of men and on community of goods. National distinctions are no longer to exist in this, nor is any recognition to be given to the authority of the father over his sons, of public power over the citizens, or of God over men united in civil commonwealth. All such ravings, should they be carried into effect, must culminate in a tremendous social convulsion, such in fact as is now experienced and felt by not a small part of Europe. Precisely a similar condition of affairs, We are aware, is ambitioned among other peoples. The masses are wrought into excitement by the fury and audacity of a few, while grave disturbances break out in many places.

Meanwhile, pre-occupied above all else with this course of events, We have not failed to renew in the sons of the Church a sense of their duty, whenever the occasion presented itself. This purpose, for example, We but recently accomplished through the letter addressed by Us to the bishop of Bergamo and also to the bishops of the Venetian province. And so now, prompted by the same motive, namely to recall to their duty those of our own fold, however many, who earn their bread by the labor of their hands, and to preserve them immune from the contagion of socialism, than which nothing is more opposed to Christian wisdom, We have with great solicitude placed before them in a particular manner the example of St. Joseph, that they may follow him as their special guide and may honor him as their heavenly patron.

Benedict now begins a special encomium of St. Joseph as patron of the workingman.

It was he, who in very deed lived a life similar to theirs; and for this reason our Lord Jesus Christ, though in truth the only-begotten Son of the Eternal Father, wished to be called the "son of the carpenter." Yet how numerous and how great were the virtues with which he adorned his poor and humble condition! Among all these virtues none was wanting to ennoble the man who was to be the husband of Mary Immaculate and to be thought the father of our Lord Jesus Christ.

Let all persons, then, learn from Joseph to consider present passing affairs in the light of future good which will endure forever, and find consolation amid human vicissitudes in the hope of heavenly things, so that they may aspire to them in a manner conformable to the divine will—that is, by living soberly, justly, and piously. In reference to the labor problem it is opportune to quote here the words which Our predecessor, Leo XIII of happy memory, uttered on this question, for they are such that no other words can be considered appropriate.

Here follows the paragraph from Leo XIII's encyclical, *Quamquam Pluries*, concerning "Considerations . . . for their welfare," as on page 149. Benedict then returns to the devotion to St. Joseph as a means of fostering devotion to the Holy Family and therefore of strengthening holy family life.

With the increase of devotion to St. Joseph among the faithful there will necessarily result an increase in their devotion toward the Holy Family of Nazareth, of which he was the august head, for these devotions spring spontaneously one from the other. By St. Joseph we are led directly to Mary, and by Mary to the fountain of all holiness, Jesus Christ, who sanctified the domestic virtues by His obedience toward St. Joseph and Mary.

We desire, then, that these marvelous exemplars of virtue should serve as inspiration and as models for all Christian families. Even as the family constitutes the foundation of the human race, so by strengthening domestic society with the bonds of purity, fidelity, and concord, a new vigor and, as it were, new lifeblood will be diffused through all the members of human society under the vivifying influence of the virtue of Christ; nor shall the result consist merely in the correction of public morals but in the restoration of public and civil discipline itself.

Therefore, full of confidence in the patronage of him to whose providence and vigilance it pleased God to entrust His only-begotten Son as well as the Virgin most holy, We earnestly exhort all the bishops of the Catholic world that in the Church's present need they should induce the faithful to implore more earnestly the powerful intercession of St. Joseph. And since there are many ways approved by this Apostolic See for venerating the holy patriarch, especially on all Wednesdays of the year and during the month consecrated to him, We wish that at the instance of each bishop all these devotions should be practiced in each diocese as far as possible.

Then, too, since Joseph, whose death took place in the presence of Jesus and Mary, is justly regarded as the most efficacious protector of the dying, it is Our purpose here to lay a special injunction on Our venerable brethren that they assist in every possible manner those pious associations which have been instituted to obtain the intercession of St. Joseph for the dying —such as the "Association for a Happy Death," and the "Pious Union of St. Joseph's Passing," established for the benefit of those who are in their last agony. . . .

Given at St. Peter's at Rome, July 25, Feast of St. James the Apostle, 1920, in the sixth year of Our pontificate. (*Acta Apostolicae Sedis,* 12, 313.)

* * *

One of the titles of St. Joseph which deserves to be more widely known among Catholics is his position as patron of the Church's struggle against atheistic communism. This is a logical development of his position as Patron of the Universal Church and Patron of Labor. The declaration was made by Pius XI at the conclusion of *Divini Redemptoris,* his encyclical on atheistic communism. It is noteworthy that Pope Pius issued the encyclical on the feast of St. Joseph, March 19, 1937.

## *DIVINI REDEMPTORIS*—PIUS XI

To hasten the advent of the peace of Christ in the kingdom of Christ, so ardently desired by all, We place the vast campaign of the Church against world communism under the standard of St. Joseph, her mighty protector. He belongs to the working-class, and he bore the burdens of poverty for himself and the Holy Family, whose tender and vigilant head he was. To him was entrusted the divine Child when Herod loosed his assassins against Him. In a life of faithful performance of everyday duties he left an example for all those who must gain their bread by the toil of their hands. He won for himself the title of the "just man," serving thus as a living model of that Christian justice which should reign in social life. (*Acta Apostolicae Sedis* 29, 106.)

* * *

Two obscure discourses of Pius XI present tributes to St. Joseph which deserve to be better known. Both of these were delivered on

March 19, the feast of St. Joseph—the first in French, 1928, the second in Italian, 1935.

## TWO TRIBUTES FROM PIUS XI

Between these two missions [of John the Baptist and of St. Peter] there appears the mission of St. Joseph, withdrawn, silent, almost unperceived, destined to shine forth only several centuries later—a silence which was to be followed no doubt by a resounding chant of glory, but long, long afterward. Indeed, there where the mystery is more profound, where the shades of night covering it are more dense, where the silence is more complete, truly there it is that the mission is more exalted and the ensemble more brilliant of the requisite virtues and of the merits called on by happy necessity to be their echo. This was a unique and magnificent mission, that of protecting the Son of God and King of the world; the mission of protecting the virginity and holiness of Mary; the singular mission of entering into participation in the great mystery hidden from the eyes of past ages, and of thus cooperating in the Incarnation and in the Redemption. (*Vie Spirituelle*, 19 [1928–1929], 677–678.)

This is the mystery, the secret of the divine Incarnation, of the Redemption which the Holy Trinity reveals to man. In truth, it is impossible to rise higher. We are in the order of the hypostatic union, of the personal union of God with man. It is in this moment that the gesture of God invites us to consider the humble and great saint; it is in this moment that God utters the word which explains all the relationships beween St. Joseph and all the great prophets and all the other great saints, even those who have had elevated public missions like the apostles. No other distinction can surpass that of having received the revelation of the hypostatic union of the divine Word. . . . In the case of Jesus and of Mary the angels offer them respect and veneration. And in their turn, Jesus and Mary themselves obey and offer their homage to Joseph, for they reverence what the hand of God has established in him, namely, the authority of spouse and the authority of father. Consequently, the confidence should be very great which we ought to bear toward this saint, founded as it is on such prolonged and even unique relationships with the very sources of grace and of life, the Blessed Trinity. (*Bollettino del clero romano*, 16 [1935], 57.)

* * *

The outstanding event of the pontificate of Pius XII as far as the devotion to St. Joseph was concerned was his institution of the feast of Joseph the Worker. Like so many events of this sort, the announcement at the time attracted only moderate attention that did not suggest the importance it would eventually assume.

A change in the liturgy is not the result of a decision made overnight. It is the culmination of long and careful study of suggestions made to the Holy See. Often enough, these suggestions themselves have been brought forward for years without apparent success. Even if the idea in itself as first represented seems reasonable, other factors can make it inexpedient. Prudent moderation must guide the Church in matters such as this. The selection of feasts must never overload the Church calendar with observances in a number so unreasonable that there would be a danger of substituting formalism for the spirit of genuine piety.

Another danger is that if the feasts become too many, they also become so common that they cannot be—or at least they will not be—widely celebrated and observed. In such a case they lose the effect for which they were intended, namely, to remind the faithful of inspiring truths to live by. Fortunately, in the case of the feast of Joseph the Worker the danger of these retarding factors was not present.

The feast of Joseph the Worker was first announced by Pius XII in an address given on the occasion of the tenth anniversary of the Christian Association of Italian Workers, May 1, 1955.

## JOSEPH THE WORKER—PIUS XII

From the beginning We put your organization under the powerful patronage of St. Joseph. Indeed, there could be no better protector to help deepen in your lives the spirit of the gospel. As We said then [March 11, 1945], that spirit flows to you and to all men from the heart of the God-man, Savior of the world, but certainly, no worker was ever more completely and profoundly penetrated by it than the foster father of Jesus, who lived with Him in closest intimacy and community of family life and work. Thus, if you wish to be close to Christ, We again today repeat, "Go to Joseph" (Gen. 41:44).

Yes, beloved workers, the Pope and the Church cannot withdraw from the divine mission of guiding, protecting, and loving especially the suffering, who are all the more dear the more they are in need of defence and help, whether they be workers or other children of the people. This duty and obligation We, the Vicar of Christ, desire to declare again clearly here on this first day of May, which the world of labor has claimed for itself as its own proper feast day. We intend that all may recognize the dignity of labor, and that this dignity may be the motive in founding the social order and the law founded on the equitable distribution of rights and duties.

Acclaimed in this way by Christian workers and having received, as it were, Christian baptism, the first day of May—far from being an incitation to discord, hate, and violence—is and will be a recurring invitation to modern society to accomplish what is still lacking for social peace; a Christian feast, therefore, that is a day of rejoicing for the concrete and progressive triumph of the Christian ideals of the great family of all who labor.

In order that this meaning may remain in your minds and that in some way We may make an immediate return for the many and precious gifts brought to Us from all parts of Italy, We are happy to announce to you Our determination to institute—as in fact We do now institute—the liturgical feast of St. Joseph the Worker, assigning it to the first day of May. Are you pleased with this Our gift, beloved workers? We are certain that you are, because the humble workman of Nazareth not only personifies before God and the Church the dignity of the man who works with his hands, but he is always the provident guardian of you and of your families. (*Acta Apostolicae Sedis* 47, 402.)

We do not know who first thought of the plan for the new feast (whether Pope Pius himself or his advisors), but it was an excellent decision on many scores. Probably the greatest advantage was that it "baptized" May Day. For decades the first of May had been observed in European countries as nothing more than a mere celebration honoring the workingman. The cause of labor had been espoused by atheistic communism, and under such auspices May Day became an excuse for rioting, anarchy, and the preaching of irreligious doctrines of class hatred. There was no doubt that May Day was considered a holiday; the Church's master stroke was to make it a *holyday* as well, and particularly a holyday of labor, by dedicating it to St. Joseph, himself a workingman.

This is not the first time in Church history that such a change had occurred. Christmas Day is an example. As mentioned in an earlier chapter it substituted the birth of the eternal Sun of justice for the pagan feast celebrating the "birth of the sun" at the height of midwinter. Just as Christmas annually calls attention to the Incarnation of Jesus, so now does the feast of Joseph the Worker call attention to the dignity of Joseph, husband and father in the Holy Family at Nazareth.

Another parallel exists in the case of the feast of Christ the King, celebrated on the last Sunday of October. In the encyclical on Christ the King, Pius XI made a comment which holds equally true for Joseph the Worker. The faithful, he said, are instructed in the truths of the faith and are brought to appreciate the inner joys of religion far more effectually by the yearly celebration of liturgical feasts than by any pronouncement, however weighty, of the teaching authority of the Church.

One of the reasons for this is that the Church's teachings primarily influence the mind, but her feasts affect both mind and heart. We remember, too, that a statement of doctrine can lie unnoticed amid the pages of tomes that are practically inaccessible to the average person and therefore unknown to him. On the other hand, the annual recurrence of a feast is a reminder and an occasion for popular explanation of its meaning.

In this case the meaning of the feast of Joseph the Worker is twofold: first, the dignity of St. Joseph, and second, the dignity of labor as personified in St. Joseph. The feast replaced the former Solemnity of St. Joseph, which had been celebrated since 1913 on the third Wednesday after Easter. As far as St. Joseph was concerned, the Solemnity had been a worthy mark of honor in itself, but it did not receive much popular notice. It could not be observed widely outside monasteries and convents simply because it was an obscure "third Wednesday." Joseph the Worker, however, changed all that. The public notice given to May Day has been given an inseparable connection with the religious notice given St. Joseph.

In the United States and Canada, May Day is not observed as a secular holiday as it is in Europe, and hence receives or might receive less prominence religiously. None the less, the feast of May 1 has been signaled as a fitting way to open the month of Mary with the honoring of Mary's husband. Moreover, in the years when this falls on a Sunday, the mass of Joseph the Worker will be said as the parish mass and will thus do its duty of instructing the faithful as far as St. Joseph is concerned. Still another advantage exists in that the mass of Joseph the Worker may by special indult of the Holy See be said on Labor Day in September in both the United States and in Canada. We can realize with joy that we now have a mass fitting Labor Day as never before. The resultant sanctifying of Labor Day is all to the good, both for the increase of devotion to St. Joseph and for a proper evaluation of the vocation of labor.

The list of advantages of the change can be continued even more. It is true that the feast seems inferior theologically to the more exalted and broader, though more abstract universal patronage of St. Joseph, which was the subject of the Solemnity which it replaced and which was then included in March 19. This, however, is not without its own benefit. The subject of the feast—Joseph's patronage of labor, and the dignity of labor—is much more intelligible to the popular mind because it is more concrete and closer to the material needs of everyday life.

* * *

In the last year of Pius XII's life, just seven months before he died, the Pope gave another public manifestation of his devotion to St. Joseph. He composed a prayer in honor of Joseph the Worker, to be said by workmen, and on March 11, 1958, attached to it a partial indulgence of three years.

## PRAYER TO JOSEPH—PIUS XII

O glorious patriarch St. Joseph, humble and just workman of Nazareth, who has given to all Christians but especially to us, the example of a perfect life of assiduous work and admirable union with Mary and Jesus, help us in our daily tasks, so that we Catholic workmen may also be able to find in them the efficacious means to glorify our Lord, to sanctify ourselves, and to be useful to the society in which we live—all as supreme ideals of our actions.

Obtain for us from our Lord, O beloved Protector, humility and simplicity of heart, love of work, and benevolence toward those who are our companions in it; conformity to the divine will in the inevitable sufferings of this life, and joy in bearing them; a consciousness of our specific social mission and a sense of our responsibility; a spirit of discipline and of prayer; docility and respect toward our superiors; brotherhood toward our equals; charity and indulgence for those who depend on us. Be with us in moments of success, when everything beckons us to taste the honest fruits of our fatigue; but sustain us in our hours of sadness, when heaven seems to be closed against us and the very instruments of labor seem to rebel in our hands.

Grant that according to your example we may keep our eyes fixed on our mother Mary, your most sweet spouse, who silently used to do her weaving in a corner of your modest workshop, with the sweetest smile playing on her lips. Grant that we may not lose sight of Jesus, who busied Himself with you at your carpenter's bench. Thus may we be able to lead a peaceful and holy life on earth, as a prelude to that eternally happy one which awaits us in heaven for ever and ever, Amen. (Translated from the French edition of *Osservatore Romano,* March 28, 1958, *Acta Apostolicae Sedis* 50 [1958], 335.)

* * *

Collections of papal documents typically contain solemn pronouncements couched in technical phrases. The following text is something far different. On February 19, 1958, Pius XII gave a radiocast to American schoolchildren, which was largely concerned with St. Joseph. The speech is of particular interest because throughout, the Pope exalted the role, the holiness, and the personality of St. Joseph. This address does not have, of course, the doctrinal importance of a formal encyclical or official decree, but it has great value in mirroring the mind of Pius XII and the modern appreciation of the Saint.

## TO AMERICAN SCHOOLCHILDREN—PIUS XII

Is it possible that another Lent has come around and that We are asked once again to speak to Our dear schoolchildren in America? Surely nothing pleases Us more than to talk with the young ones of the cherished flock belonging to the divine Shepherd. During the year hundreds and hundreds of children come to see Us here in Rome and out in the hill country nearby; We talk to them and often they answer Our questions. We cannot do that this morning, because you are too far away. But at least Our voice can travel across the ocean, and in one way brings Us really into your classrooms.

And what is the message it carries for you? Let Us tell you briefly. Next week you will begin the month of St. Joseph. Now We have decided this year to entrust to him the charge of all We fondly wish and hope for from you.

St. Joseph, as you have all learned at home and at school, was a very holy man. He had to be, because he was married to the Virgin Mary, the purest, the holiest, the most exalted of all God's creatures. More than that, the Eternal Father confided to the care of St. Joseph His own only-begotten Son, become man on earth, Jesus Christ. Mary was the mother of Jesus, the tenderest and most loving of all mothers; and though Joseph was not His father, he had for Him by a special gift from heaven all the natural love, all the affectionate solicitude that a father's heart can know. With Mary his wife, he shared all the joys and sorrows, the plans and anxieties that come to a mother in bringing up her child. Day after day, at home and in the carpenter shop, his eyes rested on Jesus; he protected Him against the dangers of childhood; he guided His advancing years, and by hard work and with religious devotedness he provided for the increasing needs of the Mother and the Son.

What a beautiful family life there was at Nazareth! You call it the *Holy Family,* and rightly so. In that small house you find Jesus, holy more than anyone can imagine, who has come to help you and everybody become holy and pleasing to the Father. There you find His mother, your Blessed Mother; and, as you know, from the first breath she breathed and all during the days of her life, her soul was simply one marvelous, indescribable thing of beauty, like a precious jewel whose every facet reflected clearly, unobstructed, the infinite holiness of God. And then there was Joseph, modest, self-effacing, yet exercising authority over that family. How holy he must have been! Under his fatherly protection and ceaseless, tireless care the young Boy grew into manhood, Who later on Calvary's cross, dying, would restore life to man, and draw all men into oneness through grace with Himself. With Him as their head they should then form that one big, big family scattered all over the world. You call that family the Church, the one, true Catholic Church, of which you are members, and that membership is your richest treasure on earth.

Now let Us ask you, dear children, if Joseph was so engaged heart and soul in protecting and providing for that little family at Nazareth, don't you think that now in heaven he is the same loving father and guardian of the whole Church, of all its members, as he was of its Head on earth? We hear your answer: yes. And does he not know that, oh so many of its children are terribly in need of help? They need help for their souls—the grace of repentance, the grace of perseverance, the grace of humble, unstinted surrender to the holy will of God; and Joseph turns to Jesus, of old his Boy of Nazareth, and at once graces flow abundantly for the souls of men.

They need help also for their bodies: fathers are out of work, mothers are bending beneath burdens far too heavy, children are without sufficient food and clothing and medicines when ill; and Joseph turns to you. Yes, it is to you he turns. He must look to you to aid and encourage those children, who are also your little brothers and sisters. We know you will not fail him. Your devotion to him will spur you on to make little sacrifices and big ones, too, so that the vast human family that Jesus yearns to unite in faith and charity, will know that St. Joseph is still the alert and generous guardian and protector, working now through his loyal clients. And so as We said at the beginning, with confidence We commit to him the charge to bestir the unselfish affection that fills your hearts for those who need and ask assistance.

We leave you now, dear children, but first We wish to give you a proof of the fatherly care We have for all of you. And so, with the full affection of Our heart We impart to you, to your dear parents, and all at home, to your teachers and pastors, Our Apostolic Benediction. May it draw down into your souls the strong grace of abiding fidelity to God and His Church; and never forget that St. Joseph is always standing by to protect you. (*Osservatore Romano*, February 20, 1958, *Acta Apostolicae Sedis* 50 [1958], 174.)

# 12.
# St. Joseph Begins to Come into His Own

We can appreciate something of Joseph's glory on earth by contrasting the long centuries of obscurity with the growth of modern theological doctrines concerning the Saint. This does not mean that Catholic writers have with Church approval invented new and outlandish beliefs concerning him. What has happened is an ever deepening insight into the full meaning of his vocation as head of the Holy Family. The conclusions that have lain implicit for so many hundreds of years are now being brought forward for theological appraisal and classification.

The theology of St. Joseph represents, therefore, the systematic study of doctrinal claims concerning the Saint—their basis, the objections brought against them, and the answers to such objections. In a sense it is a division of Mariology, the theology of our Lady, which in its turn is a further division of Christology, the theology of our Lord. In recent decades it has been given the name "Josephite theology" or

"Josephology," both terms which seem to have won general acceptance.

Some of the doctrinal facts concerning St. Joseph are contained in the gospel accounts at least implicitly. Others seem to flow from the requirements of the vocation God gave him, understanding it in its fullest sense. We should emphasize that nothing is explicitly defined by the Church that would refer exclusively to St. Joseph. Other teaching, however, is set forth as safe and prudent to accept and requires a respectful internal assent, such as the many points presented by Leo XIII in his encyclical, *Quamquam Pluries*.

We should not be discouraged by the fact that not every claim made for St. Joseph can be given a certain "yes" or "no" answer. In such cases the evidence is not sufficient to lead that far. Nevertheless, even the careful discussion of a moot point together with the charitable and objective weighing of pro's and con's deserves to be called an advance in knowledge. The gaps in such knowledge may perhaps be filled in later.

## Joseph's Dignity and Holiness

The theology of St. Joseph begins on the basis that Joseph's dignity surpasses that of all other men, save, of course, the dignity of the divine man, Jesus Christ. The reason for this principle lies in the providential choice of St. Joseph as the virginal husband of Mary the Mother of God, and as the virginal father or father in the spiritual order of Jesus Christ, the God-man. Dignity indicates excellence, worth, personal value. Joseph's ineffable closeness to Mary and Jesus means that he was privileged far beyond all other men. The gospels intimate and the Church by its statements and practice teaches that Joseph was not unworthy of the dignified position God bestowed on him, but carried it out to the utmost perfection.

Joseph's holiness as second only to that of our Lady goes hand in hand with his dignity. God would never have chosen him for such a position had he not possessed the holiness requisite and fitting for the husband of Mary and father of Jesus on earth. However, the unique vocation in itself advanced his holiness. By the fact that he was thrown into such daily contact with Jesus, the source of holiness, and Mary, the holiest of all human beings, Joseph inevitably made further progress toward the heights of unbelievable union with God. The example of his two charges would constantly spur him on. They loved him so, as husband and father, and sought to repay him in some worthy fashion. What better or more efficacious repayment than to pray for him? On all these accounts Joseph advanced mightily, and received holiness that surpassed even that of the greatest of the angels. The reasons are always the same. No one other than Joseph lived with Mary and Jesus in the ineffable love of the Holy Family.

There does exist, of course, the mystery of God's choice in such matters. On the one hand, the selection of St. Joseph for this task was a tremendous gift of God, for which Joseph could claim no intrinsic right. But on the other hand, God in His infinite wisdom foresaw the nature of Joseph's cooperation with His grace. We mortals are unable to assess with our puny intellects the plans of omnipotent Wisdom. We can, however, admire and believe in the existence of realities of God's making even when we see them only faintly hinted at.

Two other topics in the theology of St. Joseph concern his relationship to our Lady and to Jesus. These have already been discussed in earlier chapters and have received further notice in the commentary on papal documents of the previous chapter. From these summations we would only repeat here that the marriage to the Blessed Virgin and the spiritual fatherhood of Jesus are always the two foundations on which all other theological deductions concerning St. Joseph are built.

## Joseph's Prerogatives

Earlier theologians speculated on the existence of special gifts of grace that must have been given to a man so blessed as Joseph in a vocation requiring such complete conformity to God's will. One of the earliest questions, brought forward as early as the fifteenth century, was the discussion whether or not Joseph had been conceived immaculate, that is, whether or not he had begun his existence in his mother's womb free from original sin.

We must admit that the question was much misunderstood, perhaps because of the ignorance of the physical processes of conception. However, even putting the subject into the right perspective, the reasoned decision of the body of Josephite theologians is that St. Joseph was not given this privilege. Theoretically, Pius IX's definition of Mary's Immaculate Conception did not rule out the possibility that someone other than Mary might have been given the gift of freedom from original sin. All evidence, however, indicates that Mary alone was conceived immaculate. Practically speaking, the body of Church theologians conclude that the privilege was reserved for Mary alone, to fit her for her unique motherhood. Sometimes the principle (applied rightly by Leo XIII in his encyclical) of the likeness that must exist between husband and wife has been claimed to apply here. The assertion has been made that if Mary was conceived immaculate, Joseph, too, should have had the like gift.

This reasoning fails in the fact that the likeness between husband and wife is not to be understood as absolute. Relatively speaking, Joseph is to be pictured as similar to Mary as possible, always however with the proper distinctions and reservations for the gifts that belonged solely to Mary. She alone was physically the mother of God; Joseph's relationship to Jesus was not physical but was restricted to the moral order. Hence, Pius XII could say in his encyclical, *Fulgens Corona,* that Mary "obtained this most singular privilege, never granted to anyone else, because she was raised to the dignity of Mother of God" (*Acta Apostolicae Sedis* 45 [1953], 580).

The next claim made for St. Joseph was that he had been freed from original sin in his mother's womb, again as a special prerogative given by God to fit him better for his later vocation as virginal father of Jesus. The basis for the assertion is the fact commonly accepted by theologians that John the Baptist was purified from original sin in his mother's womb at the time Mary visited Elizabeth. *A fortiori*, by a stronger line of reasoning, Joseph, whose vocation was so much more exalted than John's, should have had the same privilege.

To speak impartially, the argument cannot be decided fairly one way or the other. It is true that no such evidence, not even a hint of prenatal sanctification of St. Joseph exists in scripture; but on the other hand it is hardly necessary to ask explicit and direct scriptural justification for every theological truth.

Again, it has been claimed that this privilege was required by the nature of Joseph's vocation. This, too, cannot be proved. Whether one is cleansed of original sin earlier or later does not seem to be an essential element in gauging later sanctity. God's grace can accomplish in a moment whatever marvels are necessary. Our conclusion must be that *if* the privilege of prenatal sanctification was necessary for increasing Joseph's fitness for his vocation, then God bestowed it on him. Beyond this point we cannot go.

The mention of St. John the Baptist brings up the ever recurring question about the relative sanctity of John and Joseph. The particular point at issue is the proper interpretation of our Lord's words, "Indeed, I tell you, among those born of women there has not arisen one greater than John the Baptizer; yet one who is but little in the Kingdom of Heaven is greater than he" (Mt. 11:11). The Latin and some Greek manuscripts of Luke (in 7:28) give the substance of these words in a slightly different form, "There has not arisen a greater prophet."

We must keep in mind that Jesus is speaking here like a Jew of his time, using strong hyperbole to make a point. He is actually not so much interested in making a comparison of John with anyone else as in indicating bluntly that John's holiness is truly great. If our Lord's words were actually taken at their face value, then John would be greater than Mary and even Jesus—both born of women—a conclusion which cannot be sustained.

The final proof that this text does not exclude St. Joseph from his summit of holiness is the sentence that the "one who is but little" or "least" in the kingdom of heaven is greater than John. Since our Lord referred to His newly founded Church as the kingdom of heaven, He is saying in so many words that, all other things being equal, it is better to be the least member of the Church in the New Law than to be in the Old, even as one so holy as John, who was the greatest and the last of the prophets. Accordingly, the theological deduction of Joseph's holiness and dignity is not contradicted by these or any other words of Jesus.

The requirements for St. Joseph to carry out his vocation fittingly seem to call for other gifts in this regard, especially those of sinlessness. This does not mean that he had lost the ability to sin; it does mean that God would have surrounded him with such riches of grace that he would never have deliberately consented to mortal or to venial sin, and probably, never to semideliberate venial sin as well. By the grace of God even the slightest base desire of concupiscence was restrained or ligated in him.

The reason for these conclusions is that Joseph is so intimately linked with the absolute purity of heart that existed in Jesus and was mirrored so faithfully in the Immaculate Heart of Mary. If Joseph had sinned at *any* time in his life, even in the slightest degree, this would have been a disgraceful flaw in one so close to God. We must conclude on this score that if we find it difficult to conceive such sinlessness as existing in St. Joseph, then the fault is on our side for failing to evaluate at its proper perfection his relationship to Jesus and to Mary. Throughout, he would not have received gifts automatically necessitating his consent. His free will on its part would have given its full cooperation to the grace of God. Joseph truly earned his freedom from sin by means of a martyrdom of self-love beyond the scope of our imagination because it was second only to that of Mary.

The final point brought forward with so much emphasis today concerns the assumption of St. Joseph, the question whether Joseph is now in heaven with his glorified body as well as his soul. Was he given the same privilege as our Lady, whereby her body was taken up to heaven without the need of waiting for the general resurrection of the just on the Last Day?

The answer in the case of St. Joseph seems to be strongly in the affirmative. This is not, of course, defined or even obligatory doctrine of the Catholic Church, but it can safely be described as a probable theological opinion. The assumption of our Lady, unlike her Immaculate Conception, has never been considered as something exclusive to her. A rather enigmatic text in the gospel of Matthew (27:52) implies that at the time of the resurrection of Jesus, there were other bodies that rose from the dead and were united to the souls that possessed them. "The tombs also were opened, and many bodies of the saints who had fallen asleep arose, and coming forth from the tombs after His resurrection, entered the Holy City and appeared to many." If these words do not describe a resurrection from the dead granted to certain privileged souls of the Old Testament and anticipating the resurrection of the Last Day, then we would have to suppose that these "resurrected" ones died again, and then returned to their burial-places. On several scores, notable difficulties can be brought forward against such an assumption.

Accordingly, if the privilege of an early resurrection of the body was granted to "saints" of the Old Testament at the time of Jesus' resurrection, certainly St. Joseph would seem to have been among their number. We are told by Jesus Himself that the reception of His body and blood in the Holy Eucharist is a pledge of eternal life and a promise of the resurrection of the body (Jn. 6:54). If such physical proximity to the sacred humanity of Jesus via the sacramental appearances would so sanctify the body of the communicant, how much more sanctified would not St. Joseph's body have been, because Joseph held Christ and embraced and dressed Him during all His childhood years and lived so intimately with Him until His manhood?

For all these reasons, then, we can prudently accept as probable that Joseph's body was gloriously brought back to life after the resurrection of Jesus, and that, body and soul, Joseph was taken into heaven with Jesus at the time of our Lord's Ascension.

## St. Joseph's Name in the Mass?

What of the future of St. Joseph in the Church and in the world? Our present era has been called the Age of Mary, because our Lady's greatness has been realized and the meaning of her vocation appreciated as never before. The emergence of St. Joseph from the shadows to which early centuries relegated him has been so striking on its part that sober writers have not hesitated to predict that the next stage of theological and devotional development in the Church will be the Age of St. Joseph. In general, his obscurity in the devotional life of the Church has been wiped out, but the full appreciation of his vocation and of his holiness still must wait for the future. Perhaps the most prominent spot where hints of the old obscurity still remain is in the mass—the repetition of the sacrifice of Joseph's God-given son on Calvary, in which Joseph's name occurs never once.

It is fully understandable that in the ages when the mass was being composed, Joseph would be passed over according to contemporary views. Those years have long since gone by. No longer can we justly claim that recognition of Joseph would endanger recognition of Mary's virginity or of the divinity of Jesus. Obscure saints are invoked in the mass, some of whom are but names in history. Even a pagan priest, Melchisedech, is mentioned in the Canon!

But Joseph's cooperation with the Incarnation of Jesus meant that he cooperated with the Redemption as well, for the one prepared for the other; and the union of Joseph's will with the will of his miraculously conceived son meant even more cooperation in the ultimate work of the Savior.

Thousands of bishops, priests, and lay people have petitioned the Holy See within the last century to include Joseph's name in the prayers of the Confession (*Confiteor*), the "Receive, O Holy Trinity" (*Suscipe, Sancta Trinitas*), the "Sharing and Venerating the Memory" (*Communicantes* within the Canon), and the "Deliver Us, We Beseech Thee" (*Libera Nos, Quaesumus*, after the Canon). Up to the present, the Holy See has taken no action in this regard. Any change of the mass is to be brought about only after prudent and lengthy discussion, and, of course, only by proper authority. It does not seem rash to say that the change will eventually be brought about, at least to some extent. Joseph's position in the Church as its official patron is too great to be passed over in its official act of worship forever. That such a change may ultimately be brought about is certainly a laudable intention in our prayers. It would mean that the example of St. Joseph would be proposed more than ever before, to the multitudes of the faithful, inspiring them all the more to ask his aid and to imitate his example in loving Jesus and Mary.

The omission of St. Joseph's name in the mass should not be cause for too much surprise when we recall that the Saint had been completely obscure in the Church for its first twelve centuries, as far as formal devotion in his honor was concerned. Even when his devotion began to develop in medieval times and afterward, he still was far from being considered in the way we look upon him today. It is only after Pius IX proclaimed Joseph Patron of the Universal Church in 1870 that the Saint was given widespread acknowledgment as second in dignity and holiness only to Mary. The very *suggestion* that Joseph's name be included in the mass is not even a century old, as these lines are being written!

That is why we have genuine cause for astonishment not at what is still lacking in adequate recognition of St. Joseph, but rather the meteoric rise of the devotion to such heights, and all in so short a time as far as Church history goes.

Yes, St. Joseph "begins" to come into his own, and the end is not yet. Some indication of the solid foundations of his cultus and of the forces which the Holy Spirit has raised in the Church to honor him can be discerned in the pioneering work of the Spanish Discalced Carmelites, who in 1947 founded the first theological periodical devoted to questions about St. Joseph, *Estudios Josefinos*. Meanwhile, a humble lay brother of the Congregation of Holy Cross, Brother André, had encouraged the faithful at Montreal to pray to St. Joseph and to erect a monumental basilica in his honor. Brother André died in 1937 at the age of ninety-two, but his work lives on after him in the Oratory of St. Joseph. Here in Canada is the world-wide center of devotion to the Saint. In 1951 the Oratory founded its Research and Documentation Center, to collect all literature on St. Joseph and to encourage serious study in his cause.

The pilgrim who visits the Oratory of St. Joseph at Montreal learns from what he sees. In this hallowed spot Joseph has *already* come into his own, bringing the faithful all the more close to Mary and to Jesus.

# Epilogue
# St. Joseph As I See Him

As a reader you have a perfect right to say to yourself as you read the title of this epilogue, "One man's opinion—what is it worth? To know St. Joseph as he actually was, is far more important than to think of him as he exists in someone's imagination."

The objection would be correct in every sense where the "one man's opinion" is so subjective as to change the picture of St. Joseph given us by the gospels. Take away the outlines of the character of the head of the Holy Family, and what is left is no longer St. Joseph, no matter how beautifully the sentences might read.

We have attempted in this book to stay strictly within the limits of the accounts of Matthew and Luke. From these sources we had a true picture and a many-sided picture—so many-sided, in fact, that different facets of Joseph's character may have impressed themselves on different readers with varying emphasis. You may have one impression; I may have another. Both of us would be correct although incomplete. Each of us would round out our subjective picture with the details suggested by someone else. And that is where the value of an "as-I-see-him" account exists.

The following concluding observations are not necessarily original. Some of them have already been suggested in the preceding pages, but to return to them here has its value. For example, fifteen centuries ago St. John Chrysostom glowingly admired Joseph's faith, his uncomplaining obedience, and his absolute freedom from jealousy in selfless love for Mary. That practically set the pattern for later writers and preachers. Today we still emphasize the picture of the just man Joseph, obedient and believing; and such has been part of the picture of this book.

I personally find St. Joseph most appealing as the "human," the lovable saint. Frankly, I am frightened by the terrible austerities related of some of the saints. Perhaps the details of their lives have been cast in so grim a light because some early biographer conjured up an idea of a plaster-cast saint, deliberately "touched up" according to how such a one should act. In that case we can only hope that later hagiographers will rectify the well intentioned but misguided inventions and misplaced emphases of previous centuries.

Nevertheless, even discounting possible pious exaggeration, there still are many instances where we can only admire generosity but for prudent reasons cannot imitate it—and sometimes we will find it difficult to love. Take the case of the saint whose biographer describes him in perpetual prayer as a child, shunning games, and singled out from the beginning with what would seem to be ostentatious piety; later, *always* brilliant in study, *never* "wasting" a moment for recreation or play or banter, *never* speaking except when absolutely necessary, *always* eating the worst food and that in scantiest amounts, *always* claiming that "a word with men is a word stolen from God"—how indeed can the ordinary Christian even in the best of intentions imitate a man such as this? For the average person the dangers of rash, singular pietism exist just as truly as the dangers of spiritual laziness. The reasonable use of bodily pleasures is evidently part of the plan God has built into His order of creation.

Note well that I do not intend to criticize the austere saint, but I do make the point that he is difficult to imitate. In the providence of God a direct imitation of his conduct would be contrary to the duties of the ordinary states of life in which most people live. Actually, what ultimately sanctifies and ennobles the actions of the austere saint as well as the actions of every holy man and woman and child is conformity to the will of God. There, ultimately, for every person lies the one rule for holiness and perfection. Even austerity, if it were for austerity's sake, would be useless because contrary to God's will. Obedience to what God wishes is the one norm that must sanctify every action.

Here is where the example of St. Joseph enters. By his closeness to Mary and Jesus, by the height of the exceptional vocation to which God called him, Joseph lived out a conformity with God's will that was second only and always to that of our Lady. The amazing thing about Joseph as well as Mary is the fact that these two holiest of all human beings were simply taken for granted as a very ordinary couple in their Palestinian hamlet. As mentioned in earlier pages, they were evidently part of the village scene, part of the chatter of the market place, part of the hum in the workshop, part of the atmosphere of love in their home.

Joseph's conduct, then, marked him out in no way as being particularly unusual. Unlike Mary whose position according to the customs of the time kept her more or less in the retirement of the home, Joseph had to go out and meet his neighbors and his customers. They accepted him as one of their own. We know, two thousand years later, what they did not guess.

This was the one man in the entire human race who, because he was chosen to be the virginal father of Jesus and the virginal husband of the Mother of God, was so highly gifted. Joseph's conformity to God's will was of the order of Mary's absolute devotion: a bloodless martyrdom of self so complete that we find it hard to grasp. Yet always, to his townsmen he was "only Joseph," the carpenter.

We saw in earlier pages that it was part of his vocation to keep the secret of the Incarnation intact. In accordance with this purpose he lived his life unobtrusively, but with the holiness that was so exalted. Here, truly, is a life that can be imitated. It has nothing in extraordinary show, but rather the ordinary duties of everyday life performed in extraordinary fashion known only to God.

St. Joseph's humanness has particular appeal because of the quandary in which he was placed when he learned that his blessed wife was pregnant and apparently he could not learn the miraculous cause.

What a common experience is misunderstanding, so common to all of us! A poorly chosen word, accidentally uttered, not even seriously meant; reactions from chronic sickness or fatigue that defy explanation to the friend whose feelings they hurt; perhaps even the best of actions performed with the best of intentions, yet somehow leading to a wrong interpretation—all these and similar instances can lead to misunderstandings between the dearest of friends, be they blood relatives, husband and wife, comrades, benefactors.

And in the case of Mary and Joseph, let us never forget, the misunderstanding was directly traceable to the miraculous action of God. God had His plans for letting it happen, because Joseph's perplexity over Mary is one of the greatest proofs of Mary's virginal motherhood as we mentioned earlier. But at that one agonizing moment when Joseph first realized his dilemma, there was no angel to soothe the heartbreak of the just man. God let him suffer, just as He let Mary suffer, until in the inscrutable plans of God's love the angel did come with the message that brought together again these two hearts that loved each other so much.

The conduct of Joseph and Mary during the time of the misunderstanding is again so striking—and so imitable. Mary could only keep silence, we recall, concerning the secret of the Incarnation. We do not know why, but evidently she felt it had to be. And Joseph's conduct? Here is the one moment in his life when he almost comes into his own among the writers of early centuries. We saw in this book how they normally kept him in the background, probably fearing that his unique position as father and husband would be looked at in the wrong light. But on the subject of his actions while perplexed over Mary, they search for the strongest language to give worthy praise to Joseph, the just man.

No rancor in Joseph's heart, no wounded jealousy, no hatred, no desire for revenge, no encouraging of evil suspicion for which the cause apparently existed. By law he is not permitted to condone an unfaithful wife; his wife is pregnant, he knows, and not by him. He knows the white heat of her love of God that inspired her together with him to make theirs a sacrifice, a virginal marriage. Joseph can only seek to do what is right, to be fair and generous to the one he loves. Truly we have the right to have called this moment in Joseph's life a black Gethsemane when God seemed to be taking from him a love which for its selflessness has become the model for family love for all centuries to come.

The lesson for us from Joseph's misunderstanding is ever so clear. For us, too, in cases of misunderstanding, there should be no rancor, no wounded jealousy, no encouraging of evil suspicion. Joseph the just man had recourse to prayer—so must we. In God's providence Joseph was answered by an angel—and that will hardly happen in our case. *But we will be answered.* How, we do not know, nor when; but on the word of Jesus, our prayer, like Joseph's, will somehow bring our misunderstandings to the best outcome for God's glory, for our own greater good, and for the good of those whom we love.

There is a possible complaint or subterfuge that might still linger in our mind. Was not the misunderstanding of Joseph and Mary more or less something make-believe, because they were so holy; and after all, it didn't last too long—perhaps two weeks at most?

The answer is that what was lacking in duration most certainly was compensated for in intensity. God has not shown Himself sparing in asking those who are near Him to share in the suffering that redeemed the world on Calvary. Mary and Joseph, because closest to the Sacred suffering Heart of Jesus, suffered most. We do not have the slightest justification (as we have repeatedly noted in the preceding pages) to suppose that their life was one of absolute unruffled bliss, simply because they were the saints of saints. But they were happy, we know that, too—happy in their love for each other and most of all in their united love for the son God had given them.

"St. Joseph as I see him"—that was how we began this epilogue. How do *you* see him after having read this book? What impresses *you* most in his life? You have the picture before you of the one man in the human race worthy to be loved by Jesus as father, worthy to be loved by Mary as husband. Does not that make him worthy to be loved and imitated by us in the love we bear toward the Sacred Heart of Jesus and the Immaculate Heart of Mary?

# Topical Index

Ambrose, on austerity, 110
Aquinas, Thomas, on cheerfulness, 109
  on goodness of marriage, 42
  on perfection, 29
  on pleasure, 25
  on purpose of St. Joseph's marriage, 37
Augustine, on cheerfulness, 110
  on genuinity of St. Joseph's marriage, 34
  on parallel between virginity and marriage, 54
  on respect for virginity, 55
  on St. Joseph's fatherhood, 105

Billot, Cardinal, on St. Joseph's fatherhood, 79
*Bonum Sane,* 153
"brethren of the Lord," 46, 50

cheerfulness, 109
  of Jesus, 112
Christmas story, details, 76
Chrysostom, John, on austerity, 110
  on St. Joseph's faith, 176
churching of women, 90
Clemens, A., on necessity of love, 39
Colombière, Claud de la, act of trust in God, 106
confidence in God, 106
conformity to God's will, 103

death, fears of, 125
discouragement, cures for, 69
  from impossible goals, 25
*Divini Redemptoris,* 156

emotional maturity, 96
emulation, virtue, 85
envy, 85

Faber, F. W., on loss of Jesus, 100
faith, of Joseph and Mary, 10
  lesson of, 4
fatherhood in general, 80
fears of death, 125
*Fortune* magazine, on sacredness of body, 43
*Fulgens Corona,* 168

gratitude to God, 131
guilt feelings, 64

Hidden Life, 114
*History of Joseph the Carpenter,* 17
Holy Family as model, 150, 155, 163
*Holy Virginity,* 54

*Imitation of Christ,* 21
impurities, legal, 89
*Inclytum Patriarcham,* 139

jealousy, 85
Jerome, on St. Joseph's doubt, 63
  on "first-born," 46
  on St. Joseph's virginity, 50
Jesus, birth date, 15
JOSEPH, ST.
  age, 14, 51
  age in legends, 16
  assumed into heaven, 170
  chronology of life, 15, 36, 57, 89, 98, 115, 124

compared to John the Baptist, 169
compared to Joseph of Egypt, 147
death, 124
dignity and holiness, 137, 139, 143, 166
doubt, 57, 178
emotional maturity, 96
and exile, 88
faith, 10, 95
family background, 12
fatherhood, 75, 80, 137, 144
fatherly titles, 78
genealogy, 12
genuinity of marriage, 33
hidden life, 114, 150
holiness and dignity, 137, 139, 143, 166
humanness, 177
immaculately conceived? 167
joys with Mary, 107
and labor, 153
love for Mary, 38, 84
marriage, 33, 144
  ceremonies, 34
  as model for others, 43
name introduced into mass? 172
obedience, 95
obscurity, 115
  reasons for, 18
papal pronouncements, 135
patron of happy death, 156
  vs. atheistic communism, 156
  of universal church, 117, 136, 138, 146, 148
  of workmen, 148, 154, 161
prayer after October rosary, 149
prerogatives, 167
protector, 117
purified in mother's womb? 168
reality of life, 31
reasons for marriage, 36
  obscurity in Church, 18
  reflections, vii
receives proper honor, 165
second only to Mary among creatures, 144
theology of, 165
trade of, 120
trial of, 101
trust, 100
universal patron, listings, 117
virginal marriage, reasons, 49
virginity, 45
  and fatherhood, 83
  legends, 49
vocation, 1, 139, 157
widower? 50
the Worker, 158
  prayer of Pius XII to, 161

joy of Joseph and Mary, 107

legends, on age of St. Joseph, 16
  on virginity of St. Joseph, 49
levirate marriage, 13, 35
love of Joseph and Mary, 38, 84

Magi, star, 91
marriage, goodness, 40
mass of thanksgiving, 133
Masure, E., on perfection, 30
misunderstanding, conduct during, 178

*Nativity of Mary, Gospel of*, 59
*Neminem Fugit*, 150
Neri, Philip, 113

obscurity, value, 115
Origen, on "brethren of the Lord," 50

perfection, misunderstandings, 29
piety, intelligent, 21
Popes
  Benedict XV, 153
  Leo XIII, 33, 38, 84, 140, 150
  Pius IX, 135, 139
  Pius XI, 156, 157
  Pius XII, 54, 158, 161, 162, 168
*Protoevangel of James*, 16, 51
providence of God, 95
Pseudo-Chrysostom, on St. Joseph's doubt, 63
*Pseudo-Matthew, Gospel of*, 16, 51

*Quamquam Pluries*, 33, 38, 84, 140
  quoted in *Bonum Sane*, 155
*Quemadmodum Deus*, 136

Rahner, K., on St. Joseph's doubt, 61

scrupulosity, 64
star of Magi, 91

Tanquerey, A., on perfection, 29
Teresa of Avila, on intelligent piety, 23
thanksgiving to God, 131

Vatican Council, 24
venial sin, avoidance of, 27
virginity, goodness of, 53
  of Mary, 45

will of God, 7, 103

zeal, 115, 120